What people are saying about

Folkloric American Witchcraft and the Multicultural Experience

Via Hedera has written the sort of deeply-thoughtful-yet-instantly-accessible book I wish I had written. I am thrilled, however, that it is her inimitable voice we get from the page as she unpacks the folklore of North America with a deft hand and shows how richly the veins of magic run here. She fearlessly invites us to make magic using the tools at hand, rather than seeking exotic and esoteric magics from elsewhere. Anyone who has felt the tug of an old story saying "there's more here than you think" will find themselves scribbling in the margins page after page, inscribing READ MORE! and TRY THIS! This is a remarkable book from a remarkable talent, and an absolute must-have for folkloric witches everywhere.
Cory Thomas Hutcheson, New World Witchery, author of *Fifty-Four Devils: The Art & Folklore of Fortune-Telling With Playing Cards*

Via Hedera is one of the most important voices in American folk witchcraft today and this book is a must read for anyone interested in the subject. Combining carefully researched historic folk magic and contemporary issues and practice 'A Crucible At A Crossroads' speaks to what modern American folk witchcraft is and can be. Truly essential reading.
Morgan Daimler, author of *Fairycraft and Travelling the Fairy Path*

Via Hedera is a wealth of knowledge on American folklore traditions. I enjoy reading her blog and I was delighted to hear that she has written a book. This book is packed full of lor~ ~
history, and should have a home in your magic~
Loren Morris, Primitive Witchery

This is great, it is giving people a historical and cross cultural experience of American witchcraft and inspiration for their future in witchcraft.

Marcus McCoy, *Verdant Gnosis Volume 1, House of Orpheus, Troll Cunning Forge*

Via Hedera. The woman is a creative force of nature, harnessing the imbas only shared with poets and artists throughout time. Her curiosity has led to incredible insights for me. Her research is a very real contribution to American and New World Witchcraft. Her artistic vision is a wonderment, as Via Hedera brings to life devas and spirits from the verdant current to the forefront with genuine integrity and sensitivity. I have been honored to call her peer and friend, only to also become a patron of her work. If this book is anything like the sample I read, I have no doubt it will be added to my private collection.

Fawn Hexe, webmistress of Psychopompgroupie.com and Psychopomp Groupie Podcast

Folkloric American Witchcraft and the Multicultural Experience

A Crucible at the Crossroads

Folkloric American Witchcraft and the Multicultural Experience

A Crucible at the Crossroads

Via Hedera

MOON
BOOKS

Winchester, UK
Washington, USA

JOHN HUNT PUBLISHING

First published by Moon Books, 2021
Moon Books is an imprint of John Hunt Publishing Ltd., No. 3 East Street, Alresford
Hampshire SO24 9EE, UK
office@jhpbooks.net
www.johnhuntpublishing.com
www.moon-books.net

For distributor details and how to order please visit the 'Ordering' section on our website.

Text copyright: Via Hedera 2020
Images copyright: Via Hedera and Andrew G. Jimenez

ISBN: 978 1 78904 569 7
978 1 78904 570 3 (ebook)
Library of Congress Control Number: 2020930638

A CIP catalogue record for this book is available from the British Library.

Design: Stuart Davies

UK: Printed and bound by CPI Group (UK) Ltd, Croydon, CR0 4YY
Printed in North America by CPI GPS partners

We operate a distinctive and ethical publishing philosophy in
all areas of our business, from our global network of authors to
production and worldwide distribution.

Contents

Acknowledgements   viii

Preface: The Approach of This Work   1

1. This American Witch   9
2. The Witch Defined   19
3. The Sources of American Witchlore   39
4. Witch Blood   57
5. Tricks, Projects, Fortunes, and Charms   75
6. Hags Riding with Familiars   99
7. A Green Heart   111
8. Ancestral Challenges   131
9. Forging a New Path   141

Footnotes   150

Sources   157

Recommended Reading   163

About the Author   165

Acknowledgements

I acknowledge that I live and work on the traditional territories of the Coastal Salish people; that I live on Duwamish (dxʷdəwʔabš) land and recognize their stewardship of their ancestral home.

This work is for my mother, who taught me that our words have power and to *leave no living enemies*. For my sweet, loving father, who will be praying for my heathen soul. For Bub and Kendra, who keep me going every day. To my partner Andrew, for choosing to follow me down this crooked path. For my *tía* Virginia who taught me to receive the spirits, Auntie Dawn for bringing fairy magic into my world, and my mentor Missa for teaching me that art *is* magic. And for my friends Morgan Daimler, Fawn Hexe, Rusty Sullivan, Nick and Robin Italiano, Shirley Lenhard, Ann Witt and John E. for supporting and inspiring me; for being the best darn folk this side of the pond.

To the Land and the Bones...

And to you, Brigid the Poet, for the fire in the head.

Witchcraft was hung, in History,
But History and I
Find all the Witchcraft that we need
Around us, every Day —
- Emily Dickinson, *Witchcraft was Hung, in History*

The Approach of this Work

Being American means many things to many people. We don't agree on what it means and neither did our ancestors. There's a lot to unpack in the annals of American history and most of those narratives are seen by every American in their own particular way. One thing our early American ancestors agreed upon within their own cultures and within this newly emerging culture we call the United States was the existence of *witches*. Every country had its witches; they are part of the folk magical mind and cannot truly ever be forgotten in the fearful mythologies of man. This country was and still is full of magic, and witches too.

The New World was a bloodbath; war and uncertainty, disease, displacement, and enslavement, and the fires of those cross-cultural fears culminated in an explosion of folklore regarding magical forces and those who were in league with them. We developed an entire array of folk magical charms, rituals and superstitions that permeate even the most innocent aspects of our lives and more often than not, that folklore is shared across cultures and regions in America, and has become fundamentally unique, all our own.

Our vein of the Western Magical Traditions comes from one complex history, one that no single person can answer for. I approach this work from the point of view of those who are multiracial in America, our small voice remaining unaccounted for widely in the occult literary world - a true shame given that witchcraft in the Americas was an inherently multicultural experience. The folk magical religious traditions that developed here are something to behold, a fascinating array.

My American experience has been shaped by my ancestors,

my community and my country as a whole; I am a woman of color whose ancestors have lived on this land so long the roots get lost in the changes of time. I speak as a witch who seeks to promote the magical traditions of my ancestors and the witchery they brought here; from Africa, from Europe, from Asia, from Turtle Island - because for some Americans, like me, this is who we are and all we know. My work here going forward is not to rile controversy by proclaiming what's right and wrong, I seek to discuss the multicultural experience that built the folk magical traditions across the country.

This isn't the space for gate-keeping and racial politicking. This isn't a space for militancy, extremism, "racial-purity" or segregation. If you've come for definitive statements on race in America, look elsewhere. This is about that magic forged between people. This is a space for the self-identified witches of the New World whose ancestors came here from different countries, whose folklore shaped the foundations of American mythology.

The superstitions, folktales, and general folk magic practices of post-Colonial USA, and really, all of North America is a syncretic blend of cultural traditions primarily from Europe, Africa and the Americas themselves, and quite soon after, East Asia, and the whole of the world. Over time, what once began as separate legends, mythologies, and folk magical superstitions amalgamated into a general collection of folklore from all kinds of people from all over the world who had settled in the regions of the New World.

The folklore of America comes from Armenia and Germany, France and Senegal, China and Congo, Sioux and Salish - it comes from all over the world and has found its way into our general lore and has influenced our ideas of *witchcraft*. Do most people know where lucky pennies come from? Or why jack o-lanterns exist? Or even *who* brought the tricky rabbit as we know it into our story telling, fables, and media? Most Americans don't ever wonder about why silver bullets kill werewolves or why witches love Halloween, they just know that it's part of their culture, it's what they heard growing up. We can't always account for our superstitions about stepping on cracks or walking under ladders any more than we wonder why we keep little luck charms on our dashboards or hanging from our windows. We knock on wood and we don't speak ill of the dead. There are many Americans who always open a window or cover a mirror when a loved one dies. Some things we do because we grew up doing it, and other things we do because some of us know that the world is one inhabited by seen and unseen spirits and powers beyond reckoning.

Magic is steeped into our lives and the traditions of our families, communities, households, and selves. This magic of the common folk that has traversed the country and found its way into our entire culture has developed a compendium of resources from which Western witches are building their *own* traditions, ones that speak to *their* American witchcraft experience. This is where folkloric witchcraft movements and traditions are born; from the migration of spiritual information across the world to the Americas where a new wave of Western Magical Traditions was forged at the crossroads of clashing cultures.

Authors like Aaron Oberon, Cory Hutcheson, Lee Morgan, and Jake Richards are changing the landscape of what it means for witches in the New World to establish occult traditions based on our own land, experiences and culture just as people in the Old World established their occult traditions based on the magic of the world as *they* knew it. Folkloric traditions are just one vein of the Western Magical Traditions; this country is a culture that *loves* tradition (even when we seek to change them). It makes sense that the occult zeitgeist of the Americas today is moving past ceremonial occult magical traditions and into the folkloric, the low magic; it's accessible, it transcends racial boundaries and gives us a sense of authentic identity of our ancestors and our community.

I want to lend a voice to an overlooked and yet infinitely valuable demographic of the witchcraft revival of the 21st century; multiracial Americans and our multicultural world of magic. I'm not speaking to you from the perspective of a single culture. I can't speak for the black experience, the white experience, the Latino or Native experience. I *can* speak to you from parts of all these worlds but only from where I'm sitting in-between them. I'm speaking to you as a racially ambiguous person who passes for many things and nothing at the same time... a very complicated yet common dimension to exist in.

America is one country, but we don't all occupy the same America on a social level. Culture, sexuality, "race", and religion create different worlds within America that are difficult to navigate. We are not all sharing the same cultural experience, we are not all experiencing the same struggles socially, racially or economically but we do share deep roots, and more importantly, we share a responsibility to be better than our ancestors. This means allowing each other the space to speak from our own American experience, to be fairly represented in this great patchwork of history.

I'm speaking to you as an American whose experience was shaped by the syncretic folk magic and spiritual systems of the people around me, and those people come from families who have long lived in North America, have long mixed, adopted and migrated and immigrated, and who represent the spectrum of colors, religions and racial identities across the land.

This work is for the in-betweeners, the people of this New World who were born from the synthesis of cultures and who live with an identity that embraces and reflects the merging of people, and their magical traditions. Some of us 'pass for black', some of us 'pass for white'; some of us grew up with people like us, others grew up set apart from anyone with a similar identity. But all of us are living an American experience, which by its

4

virtue and nature is a mosaic, a fruit bowl, a kaleidoscope, or, a melting pot of cultures of the world depending on who you ask. I approach this as a folkloric witch who loves the land and the bones of my ancestors who rest within it. I speak to you from Turtle Island, from the New World, from the heart, about the folk magic and witchcraft at the crossroads of the New World; a diverse magical experience.

Words Have Power

Canadian and Mexican folk magical history deserve a work all their own by people who can approach from *their* broader cultural perspective. I have no such experience with the magical heritage of the North and only a limited knowledge of the folk magic of Mexico, and only as it manifested in the American Southwest. I leave it to my brethren in the other countries of the New World to elaborate on their folkloric heart. The Americas is a vast territory, and what goes on outside of the mainland is a different story. Here, I will be focused on mainland America (United States) and other related territories within the Americas. I will also be conscious of the terms I use regarding culture in relation to magic:

> *Race* is a social construct that is generally used to highlight the phenotypic differences between people of different continents; a concept which was promoted heavily in America in an effort to classify humanity on a scale, for the purposes of justifying colonization and human ownership. The result of the systematically ingrained classification of humans by "race" and thus, by superiority, manifests in America today, as our way of separating people based on their color and the general region of the world their ancestors developed their features. It is not a system I wish to promote and I will not be using that term to highlight our differences.
>
> *Multiracial* identity is one of the many classifications of

the self and one's culture that denotes having parentage that is a mixture of what we consider to be "races" in America. It's an imperfect term for an imperfect world but it means something to Americans - for white people who have no idea where in Europe their ancestors could have come from, for black people who have zero clue where in Africa their ancestors came from (and this is the case for many Americans) *multiracial* can simply define the existence of being of unknown European, Asian, Indigenous/Aboriginal, Pacific Islander or African descent in some mixture. The term *"mixed-raced"* is loaded and not everyone is fine with the term.

Multiracial Americans of all mixtures have a long history of stigmatization, fetishization and discrimination based on their "other" status. America, up until my own parent's lifetime, had codified laws regarding "mixed-raced" people and who they were allowed to identify with. It was neither trendy nor socially acceptable to procreate outside of one's "race" throughout all of American history, and it was *especially* discouraged between white and black Americans - so much so that we had State laws and "Black Codes" barring interracial marriages until relatively recently. Even after the Civil Rights era ended, interracial relationships and the offspring of these mingling's continued to face social discrimination. It is because of the inherent social stigma against "race-mixing" and racial ambiguity that so few people are aware of how many of us there actually are, how much multiracial people have been part of American magical history, and how unique our experiences have been.

Multicultural and *multiethnic* are usually used interchangeably, but like with all semantics, plenty of people will disagree with that. For my purpose, I use multicultural to describe the American experience as it has long been described this way. We are a land where humans all converged in one place; under slavery and colonization, but also under trade and hope, in building an environment from the collective skills and passions of different kinds of people from every country; each country with its own culture, and within each culture, their ethnic groups and subcultures. This is what our country is, and preserving aspects of our ancestry while forging new traditions is what we do to preserve our unique heritage while also sharing in a singular culture as a nation, as a people.

From here on, I approach my study and celebration of the multicultural origins of American folk magic as a person of color and New World witch. This is a love letter to the magic of my homeland and the people who built it - and built me. *Up and away and through the keyhole we go...*

Chapter 1

This American Witch

Mine is a land covered in green. It is shrouded in evergreens and dense canopies and lush undergrowth. Mine is a place where rivers meet and converge, it is a place of diverse beauty in every possible way. I work along the green current, among the invasive ivy. To me, the Land and the Bones that rest within it are sacred, and is reflected in my love for this country, my ancestors and the magic they brought to this brave New World. Underneath these undergrowth forests, buried in the muck of the estuaries, settled in the mounds and hills, there are the bones of the many who came before us, the spirit of who they were still haunting our minds. For a person who appreciates the unseen world such as myself, this is a truly magical place to live, because it is full of history, and full of life.

Washington State isn't where I spent my early childhood - I'm a California girl to the bone, but I moved to the Pacific Northwest and bounced between different cultural worlds. I'm mixed, you see, a standard American combination of African, Indigenous, European and "other" thrown in. My household was a black-native household at some times, or an Anglo-black, or Mexican American depending on the year, the month. I grew up in a complicated family, the kind of family that symbolizes American culture at its finest; we're a hodgepodge mix of ethnicities and religions and ancestries and it is our shared heritage of adoption, foster-care and displacement that links us.

There may have been some moments that made me ashamed to be mixed because I wasn't, at that moment, the right color or shape for the people around me. Those moments of rejection did not outshine the moments of incredible multicultural exchange and intersectionality in which I was brought up. Growing up in East Los Angeles, most of my time was spent between four cultural groups that shaped my perception of being mixed. For me, America is by definition a multicultural experience and the folkloric "*superstitions*" and magical traditions we've developed here reflects that in every way, from sea to shining goddamn sea. It was everywhere in my upbringing, part of everything I knew.

I have no rose-colored glasses when it comes to the complexities of being mixed. Multiracial identity is a reality many people don't want to exist in. Segregation of people based on coloring and "race" is still, sadly, promoted within many communities and cultures, and it isn't any different in the USA. To be mixed *here* is to occupy a space that is both unwelcome and exotisized - you are both a mistake and a novelty. It comes with its own inherent *privileges* based on colorism and its own inherent *rejection* based on colorism. The hatred of mixing can be prevalent, powerful and inescapable in many places in the country and the world itself, but I've managed to be surrounded by people who know and are better than that.

Every one of my grandparents were a different ethnicity from the other; my siblings, their siblings, and I all have different fathers and thus have different genetic backgrounds. My mother was adopted so I spent a good deal of my life immersed in cultures that I am not ethnically related to but very familiar with. It's an old story, an American one, a magical one; people fight, they war, and they fall in love, and those emotions cross racial barriers and always have. My mother is so mixed it's taken several DNA tests and a life-long study of genealogy to even begin to unravel the incredible history - a history of violence and missing children; of tobacco plantations and moonshining; of forgotten fathers and forbidden interracial affairs with babysitters and such. It used to be a social shame, being "mixed-raced"- in fact, interracial relationships were generally unlawful in some places during our grand-parents' lifetime... but over time, Americans have come to celebrate - even to excess and pride, the different places their ancestors come from.

It's too difficult to get into the labyrinth of my genetic diversity, or heritage, beyond *American*, but I grew up walking between worlds. My lineage is complicated further by my mother having been placed for adoption from birth. Not much information was left - all the adoption agency had been told was that my very young biological grandmother identified herself as white and Indigenous and identified my mother's father as a married "mixed-black" man. She wasn't going to risk giving birth to my *"mulatto"* mother born of an affair in the deep South, that was for sure. Not in 1960's America. So, she gave birth to my mother in the Northwest where "race-mixing" wasn't always the *biggest* deal in the big city. My biological grandmother died in a tragic accident shortly after giving birth to my mother, and many answers died with her. Ma never got to meet her mother, but she tracked down and met some of her maternal biological relatives (self-identified white/Native mixed from Alabama and Florida) and learned a lot about her kinfolk and the mysteries of their complicated family.

My mother is a multiracial woman born in the 60's whose adopted parents and brother were white, whose adoptive sister was Korean, whose foster family was Cowichan, but who lived in the Mexican and Indigenous American community East of Los Angeles where my sister and I were born and raised. My biological paternal side is another complicated matter altogether for many reasons but to my knowledge they have only identified as black-Indigenous with no other mixture. The rest of my family is much more complicated; adoptees and cousins and random relations the likes of which I'm not entirely certain about their origin. We all have different skin colors, my cousins and I, and it never came up in a negative way; I think we all like being different-looking, it makes for an interesting story.

To say my childhood was *diverse* is an understatement beyond reckoning. To be honest, it was a long time before I found out most families didn't look just like mine. Imagine my surprise to find out that some people were totally ashamed to be mixed. In my life, diversity has flavored the world and fed my soul. My diet, my spiritual practices, my language all depended on what side of the family I was with. I didn't really know how I was connected to the people of the world around me, but I knew I came from the biggest, and strangest of families. It wasn't always comfortable; it wasn't always fair. There's a lot of discrimination against mixed people still, and it comes from all sides.

Like many multiracial Americans, being comfortable with myself racially was a complicated issue. I grew up surrounded by other people of similar mixtures; It was and is completely normal to see other people of mixed-white and black and Indigenous ancestry in the community, I never felt entirely set-apart. There are a lot of dimensions to *Indian Country;* it isn't just the people on the rez; it's the displaced and adopted, the enrolled and unenrolled, the recognized and the remnants, it is inter-tribal disputes and the struggle for preservation. I didn't grow up with the stigma of *blood quantum* politics hanging over my head. That has not been my experience in the Northwest. Over here, most people in the American Indian

12

community seem well aware that Indigenous-descended people face struggles related to displacement, identity, recognition, mixing and heritage; nobody is surprised by mixed people in the Indigenous community at this point because of the last 400 years of history.

Much of my childhood education in the early-late 90's was spent involved in Indigenous-centered curriculum, community and school programs because of my mother's involvement in American Indian affairs through advocacy, work in corrections in connection to United Indians of All Tribes, as well as in community engagement. This exposure allowed my sister, brother and I the opportunity to be educated by people—by family from all over the diverse spectrum of Indigenous American life. Even though my mother was adopted into a white family of almost entirely Swedish/Norwegian/Irish heritage as a child, she wound up spending much of her turbulent adolescence living with a friend's family, of white/Cowichan/Pauaquachin descent that could help her better understand and accept her mixed identity. This family is well-known in the community for taking in kids - all kinds of kids with Indigenous and Pacific Islander and mixed heritages, kids who struggled, kids who just needed family. Community is powerful and it taught me a lot about the power of connections.

Family is a choice where I'm from, and I know plenty of Americans were raised believing the same thing. I was blessed to be surrounded by people who felt the same as a matter of principle. I knew I had my feet in these different worlds every other day of my life, and I knew what it meant to be accepted or rejected at different points, but I always felt... American. I'm not crushed beneath the weight of multiple cultural identities; I'd say mixed people like me are *layered*. Being part black was culturally complicated, being part white when you are brown-skinned was conflicting to say the least, identifying as American Indian descent when the issue of *blood quantum* is a social stigma was tense ... but being American.... being a West Coast kid from the Southern California heat and the misty rains of Seattle, this wasn't too complicated.

My siblings and I have complicated parentage between us and we each have our own extended families and *other* siblings and their parents... and there's a lot of us, so what I understand to be 'family' and 'culture' is a broad statement. *Who* and *what* I was raised to consider my family was of considerable mixture and welded together by these great American experiences; *adoption, interracial relationships, multiethnic identity, civil rights, cultural preservation and the pioneering heart.*

Approaching the Crossroads

When I think of America and the absolute love I have for this country and our brothers and sisters to the North and South of the borders and on the Islands, I think of the incredible diversity of my family, of the West Coast of America itself. I take joy in my family's Southern heritage, I take joy in being racially ambiguous, I take joy in being descended from old worlds and new, in being mixed, in being ME. I take joy in growing up around Spanish speaking people and the Latin American community of the Southwest. I take joy in the collective greatness that has developed the shared North American experience.

The land and the bones that rest within it mean everything to animistic witches of the New World like myself. Our ancestors mean a lot to us, as does where we came from and who "our people" are. In truth, *my* people are humans, *my* people are North Americans, *my* people are the kind folk of the world who live around me. But in the context of American conversations; your "people" and how you identify racially and culturally says a lot about you (for better or worse). We connect *a lot* on the subject of culture and ancestry and nationality. It's not always a good thing, but it's part of who we are and how we learn about one another. It teaches us a lot in those moments and further

14

establishes social bonds.

My hope is that witches of the New World will want to reflect on their own roots right here and strive to reclaim and recreate from our own magical traditions that are shared across the country and across the human spectrum. Americans have a romanticism about the *old country*; we have this cultural perception of displacement that makes so many of us feel like the grass-is-greener in another country's garden. It's natural that a nation of immigrants and their descendants would often struggle with a sense of identity, even more so when that nation came to incredible power by horrific means in a very short period of time. Keeping track of where our ancestors came from can seem like a way to express a shared sense of displaced identity while also looking for common ground. This is why African American folk magical traditions are growing; this is why *brujeria* grows, why Southern cunning grows, why hoodoo and rootwork grows; we're a people who value our ancestry and it shapes the magic we make here.

In the context of *witchcraft,* I write about here, we sometimes struggle to reconcile the old ways with the new, the ways of one ancestor with another. We're trying to reach for a sense of connection to identity and sometimes we forget that the New World identity of witchcraft is a unique thing already, and that's where folkloric witches are following their hearts these days.

The subject of race-relations, diversity and culture is a tricky one; so many of us want to move forward, so many of us want to stay behind, and so many of us are just looking for our place in the world. We have a culture as Americans, and it is one that is steeped in superstition and magic and rituals and omens from across the globe. When you look across the whole Americas, you see syncretic spirituality everywhere you go; from the cult of Maria Lionza in Venezuela to the Santeria Lucumi of Cuba all the way up to conjure in New England. There are folk religions and spiritualities that delight in their African, Indigenous and European heritage, in the survival of spirituality under even the harshest of conditions. I love how people can hold onto their ancestors and pass their wisdom forward, I love how magic never left the heart of the people, even the magic of witchcraft. Folk magical practices played such a significant role in my childhood, it was inseparable from my everyday mundane life and permanently altered how I perceive the spiritual world. I saw the spirit in everything and that otherworldly landscape between here and there, and to this day it guides my path—it wasn't witchcraft, but it was magic.

Take up your night-riding brooms you hags; go dance with the devils at the crossroads and steal butter on Midsummer's Eve. Conjure spirits and lay tricks, shoot hairballs at your enemies and nail their tracks with iron spikes. Whisper to your familiar spirits, your roots and your stones. Go look for the magic all around you - your ancestors certainly did. And while we may see the world much more clearly and realistically today, we still have room to respect the wisdom of the spiritual world and the magic that permeates it. We fly from our bodies as moths, cats and rabbits, we fly through keyholes and up chimneys. We are said to be harmed by silver and stunned by fallen broomsticks. A beautiful blend of legend and lore that has birthed magic in the folk-mind of the everyday American.

We witches of the New World are unique, our traditions well established and defined by a powerful collaboration of Old and New World powers. We are the combination of fears and superstitions between people; we have sacred days of practice and rituals that haunt our stories from sea to shining sea, up the Blue Ridge Mountains, and down from the Cascades. The tales and superstitions that shape our customs and most sincerely held beliefs shapes our cultures in small and big ways, and shapes the way we view the mystical world, the magical world. Folkloric witches of the United States have access to a wealth of magical traditions, they create a mosaic of the land, they make up the patchwork of the American quilt; they were forged in the crucible.

Chapter 2

The Witch Defined

Maggie Alley: *"If she wanted anything, and you wouldn't give it to her, she'd take it and bewitch you. She was just witchcraft."*
James Alley: *"Everybody was scared of her."*
- Dorson, Richard M. *Buying the Wind: Regional Folklore in the United States: Mother Hicks the Witch*[1]

Witchcraft is a reaction, pure and simple; to oppression, to fear, to ostracism, to conformity, to fascism. It's a very *American* thing. We are a country shaped by fear and mysticism. When cultures meet, there is instant recognition between similarities, and one thing that all of my ancestors, all of *your* ancestors shared in, was a very real fear of the land and a very real fear of the witches who haunt it. The Puritans, the slaves and the people displaced by the arrival of *both* all held fears of witches and the mysteries of the natural world, and where there is a shared fear, there is a shared fight, and much of our folklore represents the synthesis of cultural beliefs mashed together to fight against the agents of evil that settlers saw all around them in the New World.

Africans, Europeans and the Indigenous people of early America developed a good deal of shared witchlore, some of which today cannot be traced back to a single cultural source, and it is from the syncretic beliefs of these people that traditions of magic appeared, reflecting the dominant culture of the area but always with a little hint of *something else*. Hoodoo, conjure, *brujeria*, southern cunning, pow-wow and *braucher* - any folk-magical tradition of the Americas you can name has changed significantly from whatever its original cultural source was, and now each has elements to their practice that can trace origins back to the spiritual influence of European colonizers,

Indigenous traders and enslaved Africans.

Witches could be any kind of person of any kind of religion of any kind of morality. A witch in the Western Magical Traditions was part occultist, part shaman, sometimes poisoner, always working among the spirits; a person with the power (or who is in pursuit of the power) to; conjure, heal, charm, shapeshift, project the spirit, dowse, poison and divine. They keep familiar spirits who do their work and are in congress with the dead. They differ from all the other practitioners of magic in some very distinct ways.

Of course, much of what we consider witchlore in the USA is partially inspired by the inquiries, confessions and prosecutions of the witch-trial era in Colonial America, which were inspired by their European counterparts. This doesn't invalidate the source of our lore, if anything it paints a picture of society and their fears at the time, but the information given to us from the trial confessions and legal procedures that marred the country in nearly every corner is a combination of religious hysteria, folk magic superstitions, politics and melodrama. Taking the confessions with a grain of salt, we still see a definitive and universal bond between those who practice the many crafts of magic across the board; we are all in works with the spiritual world.

This association with spirits cannot be overstated; it was written into the legal codes and procedural codes[2] that upheld anti-witch laws in the States; the witch was legally defined in no uncertain terms as a person who, among the acts of grave-robbery, image-magic and spiritual-poisoning, was deeply entrenched into the world and ways of the spirits.

That mirror universe of apparitions who come in and out of our own was supposed to be the source of a witch's powers and the object of their allegiance. Every people had its own perceptions of what separated the witch from the shaman or sorcerer. Colonial Spaniards differentiated between witches and sorcerers with witches having an explicit pact with evil while sorcerers tended to have a more casual relationship with the Devil through use of his gifts; potions, poisons, enchantments and spells. They also tended to see witches as naturally gifted with power unlike sorcerers who had to train and learn. The distinctions of magician classification existed among Spanish, Portuguese and English colonizers and their missionaries. In some colonies, witches *and* conjurors were believed to differ from sorcerers and charmers in ways; in both a legal and social manner, during the Colonial era according to Dalton's *The Country Justice;*

- **Witches** and **Conjurors** - servants of the Devil (by pact or natural inclination) who work with familiars and may perform all manner of diabolic art.
- **Sorcerers**, **Enchanters** and **Charmers** - work with magic (the tool of the Devil) but may not be in dedication to the Devil.
- **Soothsayers**, **Diviners**, **Wizards**, **Fortune-Tellers** - practice their art through the use of tools of the Devil (crystals, rings, images etc.), mainly in a professional capacity.

Of course, all of these terms became conflated; if one views all magical practices as evil, then it is all the same. *Conjurors* and *the conjuring tradition* have become conflated with witchcraft, and it isn't accurate. Conjure, a word adopted into African American lexicon from English and French, simply refers to a person who practices the summoning or spirits, entities, spells and magic in general. Today, it defines multiple magical traditions; it can refer to the simple act of conjuration of magic as the term was used in the Old World, or it can refer to the Christian folk-magical practices of some rural Americans, or, it can describe the diasporic African American religious tradition. American conjure traditions hold a deep emphasis on the Christian God more often than not, so finding a modern conjure-man who considers himself the Devil's servant would be much rarer than finding a conjure-man who prays to the Abrahamic God. The American conjuring tradition is usually framed around a distinctly Christian theology which made it an accessible practice for both black and white Americans over time. Due to the broad use of the term, the word "conjure" holds multiple meanings depending on the culture. Conflation is a common element in the witchlore of the States; there wasn't time to understand the differences, there was only time to snuff out these forces; these people who practiced the diabolic arts...

Or, as occult scholars of the renaissance like Johannes Hartlieb would put it: one who holds communion with death (necromancy), reads of flesh and bone (scapulimancy and chiromancy) and holds mastery over some divinatory aspects of the four elements (aeromancy, geomancy, pyromancy and hydromancy). The working of these *"forbidden arts"*[3] were the terms by which a witch was judged at that time. Witchcraft magic had a visionary component in the Americas; the spirit flight that those night-flying hags would take was often achieved in folklore through ecstatic dancing with the Devil, the use of ointments, oils, butters and unguents which they rubbed into their skin, with smoke, powders, potions and incantations which lifted them from their bodies or their skins and sent them through the night, through our dreams.

The primary resource of witches today are oral traditions and literature. The collections of folklore, ethnographies of the people, occult manuals and religious anthropology give us insight into the way our ancestors viewed the magical world, and how they viewed people who practiced the traditions of magic. Authors of great modern influence present us with research and narrative that give us a lot to think about in terms of defining witchcraft for ourselves:

Jules Michelet: *Think of the power wielded by Satan's Chosen*

Bride! She can heal, prophecy, predict, conjure up the spirits of the dead, can spell-bind you, turn you into a hare or a wolf, make you find a treasure, and most fatal gift of all, cast a love charm over you there is no escaping.[4]

Emma Wilby: *"The early modern British term 'witch' generally denoted an individual who was seen by others, or perceived by themselves, as being able to employ magical powers to do harm."*[5]

Richard Godbeer: *"Plymouth Massachusetts, New Hampshire and Connecticut laws defined a witch simply as, "any man or woman... [who] hath or consulteth with a familiar spirit [a devil]."*[6]

Alison Games: *Witches could be Huron shamans, Pueblo healers, enslaved conjurors and Jesuit priests. As Europeans, Americans and Africans converged in North America, so too did their ideas about witchcraft. Witches, everyone agreed, were people who performed harmful acts and threatened community order. But when societies and cultures collided on the North American continent in the seventeenth and eighteenth centuries, there was an irrevocable shift in people's assumptions about what harmful acts entailed, who was most likely committing them and how one might preserve communities ravaged by disease and conquest or formed anew out of strangers.*[7]

Marc Simmons: *In the long history of witchcraft in the Western World magicians and sorcerers have become associated in the popular mind with certain standard techniques and procedures used in the carrying out of their peculiar functions. Signing a compact in blood with the Devil and renouncing Christianity, forming cults and engaging in obscene revelry, foretelling future events, and the laying of spells and incantations upon innocent victims constitute some of the more conventional activities of witches.*[8]

Journal of American Folklore Vol XXVII: *Here are some of the things witches do in the Kentucky mountains. They transform certain individuals into horses and ride them all night, restoring the bewitched to their natural shapes before daylight: later, complaint of the jumping of ditches, fences, etc., is often made by victims.*

Witches do not confine themselves to working the black art upon human beings, but bewitch animals and inanimate objects as well.[9]

Witchcraft is a very real practice of magical and occult works. It is the use of what some call *tricks* or *projects*, *fortunes* or *spells*, *magic* or *charms* - it is the working of some spiritual force that alters the world around a person. People have always believed in witches in part because there have always been people who practice magic, and *sometimes* those people are labeled morally ambiguous people; as witches. Sometimes they **are** witches. They are not just sorcerers, shamans or cunning folk - no, a witch is someone with power who uses it as they will, in ways that the community may not benefit from.

The witch in America is deeply agrarian/funereal; a staple of witch fears throughout the Old World and New. The idea of the witch as one to maligns the domestic and agrarian efforts of their enemies is found throughout all of North America, and throughout the world. The witch is usually an agent of death, and so they are deeply interconnected with the concept of necromancy and ecstatic ritual in which the spirit leaves the body. In America, the witch is said to strip down nude, take on an ointment/oil (Southwestern) rub themselves in "witch-butter"[10] (Southeast), or take on the skin or bone of her familiar (Southern, New English) and leave her body behind, or, be fully transfigured to resemble an animal like a snake, snail or owl, fireball,[11] insect or shadow, and leaves through the smallest cracks or under doors, through keyholes or up chimneys. By whatever form, this person is famed for their otherworldly power.

These practitioners were supposed to have been sought after primarily for charms which would bring luck, protection or love, and also, for healing medicines. The witch, whether good or bad, was a valuable member of the fringes of community depending on their reputation and gifts. In the most traditional sense, a witch in the Americas was a person of power, who holds communion with the spirits, participates in the working of tricks, projects, hexes and fortunes, who may do great harm or good, and holds allegiance to some fearful force that guides them.

Each country and its people had its own folklore regarding those who use magic for *good*, and those who use it for bad or both and when these converged in the New World, suddenly, witches were *everywhere* and *anyone* could be one. The witch of the African, the European and the Native American, over time, has become a singular concept in some ways and this is what we today know of as the general witchlore of America - a combination of everyone's paranoid mistrust, misunderstanding and magical folk mind. Dark magic was everywhere in the old days.

The migration of magic was reinforced by the transmission of occult manuals in the form "chapbooks" and spiritual catalogues throughout post-Colonial America; those like *The Long-Lost Friend* and *Le Petit Albert*; materials that caught the imagination of the common folk, and can now be found within our general folklore and superstitions. The information in these small manuals would vary; some contained simple folktales or legends, others gave folk remedies and marital advice; others contained political observations of the times; some were occult manuscripts translated into English from France and Germany while others were locally printed and contained all manner of information regarding omens, fortunes, divinations and auspicious advice. These magical pamphlets found their way all over the country, being sold in shops from New Orleans to Detroit, from New English fortune shops to Midwestern hoodoo stores and were popular materials among all the different communities of America and have since shaped the practices within the American magical traditions we know.

Witches could be Christians; they could be heathens; they could be black conjurors or white cunning folk or Mexican folk healers. They were said to have rode with spirits, knew harmful ticks and, most foul of all; they knew the mysteries of the land and herbs thereof. There is an inherently animistic heart to folkloric witchcraft; the intrinsic spirit of all things magical; from the spirit flight of the witch through the keyhole, to hagriding in nightmares, conjuring the spirits within roots or haunting places with our power.

Europeans knew about witches - the earliest settlers of America - Spanish, English, Dutch, Swedes, French, German, etc., all had a "working knowledge" generally speaking, of religious backgrounds, especially respecting good and bad - angels and witches. (Aurand Jr., 1942, p.6)

What we know of as "witchcraft", along with all its assumptions and symbols and mythos in the US, is shaped primarily by the shared superstitions and spiritual fears/misunderstandings of Western European Colonizers, West African Slaves and Indigenous Americans of the Eastern seaboard and the Caribbean. When these and other groups met, their shared fear of witches only served to reaffirm, or as Owen Davies said in *America Bewitched*, "reinforce" the fears of one another.

Anti-witch practices were among some of the first ready exchanges as Europeans, Africans and Indigenous Americans all have facets of their cultural identity that was strongly rooted in a fear of those who dabble in magic or hold company with the dead. The combined mistrust and misgivings between these cultures in their initial convergence in the New World led to hundreds of years of struggle and pain - and it also created a uniquely Americanized point of view of things like magic, the Devil, spirits and witches.

So afraid, our ancestors were when they arrived here; ignorant of the land and innately hostile to the Indigenous people whose medicinal and agrarian knowledge of the land would go on to be instrumental in both African American and European American folk-medicine and folk-magical practices. While many people focus on the European roots of the Western Magical Traditions in the Americas, Europe is not at all the mother or motherland of our collective folk magical practices; this was a product of three separate continents and is people, and no one "race", religion, culture or peoples can claim authentic *ownership* over the bulk of our folk magic.

A Touch of God

There is a common Christian element in the folk magical traditions of the United States and its territories. Christian influences mixed with the folk magical customs and superstitions of those in a particular area shaped what the magic, and by extension, the witchlore of that local culture would be. In a country this large, insular communities developing unique magical traditions happens in each region in some way or another. It migrates, it moves, that's the nature of things in this country, always on the move and expanding (for better or worse). Christianity propelled this (for better or worse) and its magical influence can be felt. The *braucher* of Pennsylvania share parallels with the hoodoo folk of the Carolinas and, they both share parallels with *curanderismo* in the Southwest. Each are a manifestation of Christianity overlaid onto old folk magical customs, which over time became methodologies for magical practice and even spiritual life and conduct.

Christianity cannot be completely separated from folk-magical practices, even witchcraft; it permeates so many folk-traditions, medicine and lore that it is, in many ways, quite vital to the survival of specific magical traditions. To remove the Abrahamic god and his angels and saints from practices such as *curanderismo* and most traditions of hoodoo would not only lessen those traditions, but would fundamentally change them so much that they would not be the same practice at all. The God of Abraham cannot be completely extricated from folk-religions in America, or the charms, spells, incantations or magic within those traditions, and there's nothing wrong with that. In fact, Christianity lent its own powerful spells, spirits, incantations and charms to the witchery of the New World; something seen prevalently in the folk-traditions of rural Americans of the Northeast and South.

And each of these traditions had a dark aspect they were determined to fight; witchcraft. We are not the "good-guys" in the narratives of orthodox religions. Witches are an ever-present threat and the Church only served to reinforce the fears of the common folk regarding magic and the people who use them. It would seem like the witch is just the worst kind of villain when you put it like that but in reality, the witch was capable of great good *and* great evil, and each cultural group in early America had their own view of the matter. The distinction has always existed; even Cotton Mather drew a distinction between "white" and "black" magic if only to discourage both.[12] Eventually, the general folklore of America would report witches as both malicious or beneficial.

Christianity takes a generally negative view of witches in our country's history and of magic in general due to the nature of duality intrinsic to Western Christian practices, but magic has been successful nonetheless; infiltrating Christianity just as much as Christianity infiltrated magic, witches along with it. The American witch today doesn't need to acknowledge the Christian aspect of traditional craft because witchcraft isn't an inherent practice to Christianity, it is however a part of the fabric of the magical traditions of the Americas. Witchcraft in general is a wild and pagan thing by nature; that's why the Church so hated it. We've always been the magician that is in service to those liminal and otherworldly things, but that doesn't *always* mean the Devil of the bible...

American Devils

To learn to pick a banjo, go to the forks of the road at midnight: You will see a man; that is Satan, and he will teach you to play.[13]

What is a devil to us in the Americas? The traditional witch of lore hasn't really changed in definition over time, and if we're looking to define what witchery is in North America, the best places to start with are the sources who disseminated most of the standard witchlore we have. These were often bias and subjective points of view, a perspective that existed from the point of view of Catholicism and Protestantism, and so while they may be correct in defining *some* of the arts of witchery, they also had a vested interest in promoting witchery as *intrinsically* and *undeniably* evil. The witch wasn't *always* an *absolutely* evil figure in Western European folklore, this was an influence of the Church spurred by the hysteria of the time. Likewise, among West Africans, the belief in the intrinsic morality of the witch varied, with some seeing witches as capable of choosing their actions according to Alison Games in *Witchcraft in Early North America*;

An individual might have the power both to cause harm and to uncover and counteract it. Witches, then, were not solely or inherently evil (as European authorities believed them to be by the seventeenth century) but rather had the ability to effect good or evil. (2012, p.19)

The witch is foul by most cultural standards, and most cultural standards are bred from organized, socially acceptable religious institutions which paint most mystical/magical people in a negative light regardless of whether they are a shaman, cunning-man or witch, so we have to make peace with the unflattering viewpoints of our cultures, helping to correct the error of generalizations and umbrella statements about what witches are and how we work.

It's always important to note that most cultures, while viewing witchcraft as inherently negative, also viewed witches as people capable of great good. This is prevalent in much Southern folklore like in Tennessee and Virginia, where the lore presents the witch as either "good" or "bad" or both. This was especially true in the Southwest, where many tribes did not share their neighbors' sense of absolutism regarding individual witches. Unfortunately, even those who would normally be the combatants of witchcraft in the spiritual community were routinely faced with accusations of witchcraft (though I should note that *curanderos*, like medicine men, were seen as capable of both great good or evil,[14] and when resorting to evil, were then seen as witches among the people, but from a Church perspective, any consultation with the spirit world was witchcraft and this was legally codified for quite some time).

Because of this, the terms *cunning-man, charmer, enchanter, wizard, conjuror, witch, healer* and *shaman* have often been used interchangeably, despite the differing connotations, to describe anyone who consorts with magical practice, spirits and death. They are not interchangeable terms; they have different connotations of evil or goodness; the motivations and source of power are different. Witches were the least scrupulous of the spirited folk and that has lent to the fear around them. Evil or good or neither, the witch was a power understood across the spectrum of human cultures and across the regions of the country.

Some aspects of witchcraft tradition in America are in fact deeply Luciferian; and it needs to be understood that the perception of the Devil, "Satan" or Lucifer depends on who's asking, and if you asked some witches, they would say their view of the Devil tends to fall more on the gnostic side of things, wherein he represents freedom from oppression, the championship of willpower and wisdom. The Devil, as he is understood through American folk witchlore, was in many ways more of a trickster[15] than the supreme lord of all evil - more of a tempter of wills and dispenser of requests. The concept of a magical trickster was terrifying to Christian missionaries of the Colonial era, and so the subtleties that Indigenous and African people recognized in their (usually neutral) trickster spirits went unrecognized, and they became just another face of evil according to the Christian Europeans. Among West African descendants, a "devil" of the crossroads more closely resembles a trickster entity or liminal spirit that guides the use of magic by the people; Legba, Ellegua, Lébat, Anansi, Man-At-the-Crossroads, etc. Lords of evil? No, it depends. Just like with witches.

Demons and devils mean something entirely different to people who do not adhere to Christian theology. Classically, "daemons" were seen as capable of benevolence. Demons, being just one class of spirits are a population like any other, capable of terrible terrors and wonderful wonders. The Devil has only recently become the embodiment of all the world's evils, and only recently in history was the "devil" title assigned to every kind of dark or trickster spirit or deity we know of. The Western "Devil" and "Satan" are not always the same entity, nor is Lucifer the embodiment of pure evil. There's a complicated level of conflation and semantics at play here that shapes our perception of evil, and it depends entirely on who is interpreting the situation.

What *we* call the *Devil* in America is an amalgam of a few dozen different cultural mythologies whose darker spirits have been umbrella termed "the Devil". Pan of the woodlands is a figure passed off as the *Devil* and shared this predicament with all other horned folk deities of the woods and prey animals. Djinn of Arabic mythology, Sumerian demons and Canaanite gods, Greek Daemons and even English folk spirits all bare the stigma of being now associated with the *evil*, despite the fact that they were once given the benefit of relative nuance in their heyday. The sad nature of death, life, weather and forest deities is to be relegated to the pages of Christian history as the many faces of evil.

As Christianity fought to consolidate its power, it grew to associate all dark and mysterious and liminal entities and figures with this newly revitalized concept of *absolute* evil. But witches are not all servants of the great evil. Many of them, including those who dance with the "Devil", are not worshiping the *Satan* of the biblical narrative, rather they are consorting with old horned gods of the woods or the black-man-at-the-crossroads. He may look like the stereotypical Devil, but he is not viewed as evil personified by those witches who attend his sabbat - rather, he is cosmic willpower personified. It's important when looking into the devilish heart of witchcraft to understand that the all-evil-entity of the Christian Devil and the various "demonic" or "devilish" entities associated with him by name are not at all of similar nature or origin, and you will need to know the difference between spirits before forging a contract with any entity.

The concept of dealings-with-the-Devil crossed cultural boundaries; even African American conjurors sometimes admitted to pacts with the European devils for their ends, mirroring the sorcerous superstitions among many West Africans that witches derived their powers from evil spirits.[16] What is "evil" from one cultural perspective, and the nature of "evil" itself are up for extensive debate. Some would say that devils and demons have been good friends to them, while others would say that demons belong to a class of spirits too dangerous to be tampered with. One's perception of a spirit-pact and whether or not those deals are righteous or wrong is up for interpretation. The danger lies in linking all dark, liminal or necromantic spirits to the nebulous concept of "evil".

The old crossroads gods, like the Devil of old, before the Witch hysterias of Europe and the New World, were nuanced entities, capable of great feats of good or evil, often symbolic of man's capacity for both as well. The Devil as a trickster god, as master of misrule and choices, traditionally symbolizes the harsh lessons of our actions, the follies of hubris and the revelation of unknown things. To put him in direct odds with "good" would be ignoring the qualities of the trickster spiritual model in religion, which has always played a significant role in the teaching of dark but necessary lessons.

And so, the *devil* - however you interpret that set of spirits, is very much an aspect of traditional witchcraft in the Old and New Worlds, and to claim anything less is disingenuous to our folkloric heritage and history. The Devil, whether you like the concept or not, is important to understanding the foundation of our superstitions regarding witchery in this country. We can excuse the ignorance of our forefathers when it comes to the spirits, but we can't avoid the tradition of "devilish witchery" that the colonists perpetuated during the formative years of our country's development. The Devil, after all, isn't our enemy and is not our personification of evil, so we need to unlearn some things - not just the way history has taught us to be ignorant, but we need to change the very perception of moral duality that leads us to assign absolutes.

The reality is, if witchcraft was a simple art of the layperson, a craft anyone could fall into, then the chances are only some of those people were agents of the Devil while the rest were associated with any other manner of deity or spirit. Hell, one of the only constants in witchlore around the world is the relationship between witches and spirits - so concepts like deities and *devils* are all really secondary to the universal quality of the witch as one who serves or is served by the *spirit world*. The spirit world as an idea encompasses so much more than our own human dead; it encompasses the many entities which we call by many names but cannot truly define. Some call them fairies, demons, daemon, devil, djinn, ghosts, spirits, even aliens - whatever lies beyond the seen world, this is where witches work.

Which leads us to the matter of faith; if witches came from all kinds of religious backgrounds from various cultures, then clearly the faith of the witch will be shaped by those perspectives. If we want to cut through all the incredibly complex nuances of culture, time and religion, we can probably sum up the faith of a witch as being of the **spirits**. The universal master of the witches are the spirits; whether those of the living, the dead, the demons, the fairy, the gods, or the ancestors; witches are agents of the spirit world among others. What seems to be generally true for North American witchlore is our spiritual association with either the Devil, fairies, hags, or spirits (of nature, the dead, demons), as well as a deep association with familiar spirits/ancestors/ghosts.

For most American witches who lean towards traditionalism, our lore aligns us with spirits, plant and animal allies and yes, the Devil - but which devil we dance with depends on who we've called, and it's almost never the master of "evil". It's important that while many of us may have academic or semantic issues with the way others use the term "witch", we are all of us operating from the point of view of our own internalized biases, and since witchcraft itself is such a nebulous term, we need to be a little more patient when it comes to understanding those who share in this spiritual system - and that includes the "Devil" in witchcraft.

A Folkloric Fire

Nevertheless, there can be no doubt that folk magic functioned both as a defense against mystical attack and as a resource in the alleviation of suffering. The demand of the village peasantry for inexpensive medical care was sufficient in itself to guarantee the continued viability of magical healing practices throughout the seventeenth century. (Weisman, Richard, 1984, p.41)[17]

God and Devil aside, our idea of magical practice is shaped by the folklore around us. A *folk-witch* is the kind who practices that common magic, that "low" magic, those tricks of the land and the spirits that combine our intuition with the traditions we learn from. The traditions of magic that developed in the New World and the witchcraft that developed with it shared these general defining features:

Agrarian (pertaining to charms regarding livestock and agriculture)

Apotropaic (averting bad luck, banishing evils and appeasing to spirits)

Auspicious (generating or protecting luck, wealth and prosperity)

Divinatory (fortune-telling, soothsaying, omens and oracles)

Naturopathic (herbalism, healing charms, folk medicinal-magical rituals)

Erotic (love projects, sexual potency spells)

Funereal (abiding by the customs of the dead and mortuary folklore, necromantic work)

Transfigurative (shape shifting, skin-changing)

Ecstatic (spirit flight, sabbatic revelry, initiatory rites)

These are expressed in our folktales and stories, in our witchlore and superstitions, in our folk magical charms and conjure works, in the general occult knowledge within the Americas. We celebrate and elaborate upon our cultures and our identities, our communities and regions by expressing the many ways in which our people work. The general collected folklore has, by now, been so broadly shared and ingrained and disseminated across our media, literature, communities and families, that many people are unaware of the cultural origins or ethnic heritage of some of the superstitions which have been pervasive in their everyday life. From lucky pennies, to fountain coins, to lucky talismans; the symbolism of the broom, cauldron, black cat, apple and witch itself has a complete mythos and history in our folklore and tall tales, in our superstitions and basic beliefs.

With all these various cultures and tribes intermingling on new soil, sharing their fears and hysterics regarding a mutual belief in the realness of witches, it's no wonder that the same folk charms and lore can be found between different cultural communities in America. We share the common thread of witch-trials and conjurer fears, and the terror of bad medicine men. The witch, ever present in our imaginations and folklore is a very American symbol; as rebellious and terrifying as she was in the Old World.

Why does folklore mean so much to the rise of Traditional Witchcraft across the world today? Because it's the way we connect with how our ancestors envisioned the mysterious world and the spirits in it. Today, the practitioners of Western Magical Traditions have a great variety of information at their disposal to help them accomplish the task of understanding the history of the world's magic, and for Americans - who often struggle with a sense of cultural identity in a multicultural environment, we've come to rely on folklore as a window into the daily life of the people we come from.

Many Americans have an intimate knowledge of their ethnic

ancestry and the homelands of their ancestors - for these people, this is an important aspect of their cultural and social identity. But, for many other Americans, everything they really know, or value, or take pride in, is what grew *here*. Many Americans come from families that have been here so long that their sense of cultural identity is influenced by the pioneering and migratory histories of their ancestors as they moved across the land in settlements.

Some people think of "American" as a very unique culture with its own fascinating times in history, its own way of things shaped by the shared histories between different people of different ethnicities and cultures. The generations of American families that have grown here have traversed this great land and with it, their superstitions, customs and folklore traversed over land, and between people. We are social and syncretic; we develop connections and conflate common ideas and perceptions. It's not always good, it's not always bad. It is what it is.

Chapter 3

The Sources of American Witchlore

Witchcraft in Europe

Witchcraft in European folk belief is the most well documented we have in the Americas. Primarily coming to us from England, Scotland, Ireland, Denmark, France, Germany, Spain, Italy and Portugal, the folklore brought to the Americas from across the pond was pretty vast and represented the many very different beliefs of the Europeans. For the most part, each country of Europe that sent colonizers had its own unique history with witches and witchcraft but the view of witches was relatively similar. It was quite simple; a witch was one who was in league with devils, holding company with familiar spirits, knew the arts of deadly herbs and materials and was known to haunt and hurt those they disliked.

The witches of the agrarian-funereal folk magic of Europe, like their African and Indigenous American counterparts, were able to fly from their bodies, hex, heal, ensnare and steal. The witches of Europe, such as the Italian witches of Ginzburg's *Night Battles* could be malefic or beneficial, and they represented a more pastoral diabolic than innately evil kind of creature. This witch could be one who heals and practices a magic that, while still against the word of God, was not evil, or, they could be night-riding hags who steal your milk. The Cornish witch may be one who works the magic of toads and snails for good or evil as they see fit, and are rarely the malefic forces of evil that English witches were detailed to be in the anti-witch manuals of the Colonial era.

What Western Europe grew to know of witches evolved from their own folkish-pagan roots, corrupted by the Catholic church early on, even before the *Malleus Maleficarum* came to be used as the defining treatise on witchcraft. As each country of Europe established settlements in the New World and developed their own communities in the USA, which were typically culturally insular, epicenters of American witchlore were founded, rooted in the Old World traditions. Most witchcraft folklore we know of tends to be English and Scottish, or, Italian or German in origin - truly, all European people had their own folklore regarding witches and practitioners of magic in general, and this migrated readily to the strange New World.

In the European occult mind and in the Western Traditions of magic, there existed different kinds of people who used magic; *magicians, sorcerers, cunning folk, witches*, among others. Their magic could be high or low, their practices could be rural or systematic and witches were those most to be feared because they served the old gods of wood and wagon road and sea and stone. They were holdovers from an ancient and uncivilized world and the very idea of the witch could not be stamped out even by the immense pressure of Christian theological movements that suppressed folk magic and their superstitions. Try as the Church did, it could not kill superstition and the customs of the common people, it could only mask the beliefs and corrupt their purposes. And so, as European settlers expanded across the New World, assimilating and converting as they went, the folklore of their countries of origin passed into the folk mind of Americans and we share a lineage back to the Old World folk and their magic.

Witchcraft in Turtle Island

The witches feared in tribes of the Americas varied by tribe, by clan, by region. In general, a witch - if it existed among that people, contrasted from a medicine person (parallel to Siberian *shamans*) in that the medicine person used their gifts to serve the people, while witches could be those who used their medicine in bad ways, or, they could even be a kind of spirit; a not-altogether human entity. From the Menominee[18] of the Midwest to the Seneca of the Northeast, witches haunted the folkloric mind, differing from medicine men by their moral ambiguity. A "shaman" usually played a positive role in the community,[19] the witch may choose *not* to - but this isn't a hard and fast rule, there are always exceptions and deviations. Being that Indigenous spiritualities were primarily animistic and kincentric, the relationship between all living things was considered a sacred thing, and there were supposed to be entities which disrupt those connections - and those entities were sometimes analogous to what Europeans called "witches".

Historian Marc Simmons wrote that the Navajo and the Zuni held a relatively nuanced view of witches as people capable of good or evil;[20] they tended to be night-flying shapeshifters who used image magic in the sand or dolls of wood to harm victims. They could also remove ailments, cast an "evil-eye" on children and bring lovers together. Other Pueblo tribes had far harsher views of witchcraft and had several witch trials recorded by Hispano settlers; these trials often leading to the execution of the accused party. Among the Southeastern tribes like the Cherokee, Choctaw[21] and Seminole, witches were *serious* business and these dangerous forces could take the forms of owls, lizards, dogs and wolves to do nefarious works. Unlike the Christian European view of the witch as a person making an active choice to participate in the Devil's craft, Southeastern tribes among many others saw witches having a natural element to them, a quality from birth or childhood that marks their path.

In the Pacific Northwest, witchcraft among Coastal Salishan tribes is a very quiet and insular subject. The magical wonders of plants, animals and other entities of the land were not accumulated in written documents but rather passed on through oral tradition in the form of story-telling and it is from the stories of the coastal Salish tribes that we gather an idea of how the people viewed the magical world around them. Among the story-telling traditions of the Northwest is a variety of narratives regarding an Ogress or Cannibal witch. The story of Basket Ogress as collected and told by late Duwamish elder Vi Hilbert is a popular feature of Northwestern story-telling; her collection of the lore is some of the first written accounts of this story-telling we have and I was lucky enough to hear in both English and Lushootseed in grade-school.

The cannibal woman-witch motif stretches all the way up through Canada to the Alaskan tribes. Actual practices of witchcraft within families is a quiet thing, and not at all something that would be smiled upon. The stories of witches in the Northwest are terrifying, especially among the coastal Salish of the Puget Sound; old hags with baskets in the shape of snails[22] or made of writhing snakes who shake rotting sticks at terrified children or who trick children into their basket with promises. Some could shapeshift into great birds, and others took the form of owls. Witches in Southeastern Indigenous stories of witches were equally terrifying; owl women,[23] shapeshifters who herald death.

Unfortunately, much of what we know of witchcraft practices within Indigenous tribes are based on the tenuous observations of European settlers who often equated Native American spirituality systems with sorcery, wizardry and witchcraft (concepts which were used interchangeably in American vernacular) but the stories that survive in oral tradition today, like those I grew up with along the Duwamish river about Ogresses and Cannibal woman, have influenced aspects of our witchlore, preserved as we share the stories we hear and attribute them to their rightful holders.

Witchcraft in Africa

It would appear that witchcraft was a very serious offense among most West African cultures and that this fear of malevolent forces continued into the diaspora traditions of the Americas. Being that most African Americans are descended from slaves brought to the Americas via the Caribbean from the Congo, Ivory Coast, Cameroon, Senegal, Gambia and Nigeria, the scope of spiritual beliefs covered a wide range of people who shared some deeply rooted religious traditions which were animistic, naturopathic, and divinatory in practice. West African religious traditions tended to follow a similar divine-hierarchy structure. Between the Fon, Ewe, Kongo and other West African forefathers of most black Americans, there existed a similar structure of beliefs in the spirits, including death/liminal deities, snake gods, plant spirits and ancestors.

At the top of the West African divine order was an overarching supreme deity who typically does not interact with followers, followed by a class or court of intercessory deities to whom we pay our sacrifices and offerings, followed by totemic, tutelary, plant and ancestral spirits; and then sorcerers, witches, magicians, high priests or any manner of spiritual initiate of great power. This structure was remarkably similar to Southeast Indigenous tribes who first interacted with Africans in the New World, their shared animistic hierarchy serving to reinforce one another's beliefs.

The people and their religious beliefs were regarded with various forms of scrutiny and outright hatred when first encountered by Europeans who likened these spiritual traditions and the associated rituals of sacrifice, ecstatic dance and purification with their notion of their own culture's pestilence of *witchcraft*. History is written by the victors and so, as the Church was unkind to the folk healers and cunning folk of their *own* society, it was doubly unkind to the practices of West African Religions. Alison Games points out in *Witchcraft in Early North America* that the *"intellectual limitations and religious prejudices of European observers"* complicate our historical understanding of witchcraft as it was viewed by West Africans at the time - these misunderstandings during the Colonial era led to hundreds of slaves being accused of poisoning and conjuration.

But we do know now that West African spiritual systems held a wide spectrum of beliefs that seemed to agree that the world was inhabited by nature spirits of great wonder, ancestors in need of veneration and folk who knew the mysteries of both. And some of those people were not regarded as necessarily trustworthy with the power at their disposal, and when the cultures and their superstitions merged, those people whose powers were to be feared, were equated with *witches*.

Sometimes a witch was a person who simply exudes evil from them naturally,[24] while others were witches by way of some inherent quality of the soul; others could be tricked into being a witch and can be turned away from that path. Sometimes, like in Europe and America, witches were spirits who haunted people, places and things; they were cannibals who used magical means to attain greatness.[25]

> *European and African-derived witchcraft traditions evolved as a dual presence, confirming their significance to Anglo- and African American folk beliefs. But conceptions of the witch differed dramatically for both peoples. In the Western Christian tradition of which Anglo-Americans were inheritors, witches were seen as disciples of the devil, and theologians viewed witchcraft practice as a form of heresy. In contrast, black American ideas of witchcraft sprang from traditional African beliefs in the mixed potential of good and evil.* (Chireau, 2006, p.84)[26]

Other times, witches were cunning tricksters who were suspected of being capable of relative good or evil deeds; they could commune in great assemblies and fly with familiars. Indeed, witchcraft was part of the spiritual systems of West Africans, and the complex of African religious traditions in the Americas held on to the same notions of spirit-inhabited, witch-infested world. European superstitions and Indigenous story-telling served to reinforce the notion of witchcraft, "black magic" and the like among Afro-Americans. As always, witchcraft, being the darker art of magic, finds its way into the balance of spiritual beliefs.

These United States
North, Northeast, Midwest

The folklore that influenced the perception of witchcraft in New England was a byproduct of English, German, Dutch, Irish and French settlers along with influences from the African slaves that were working in the colonies and the local tribes whose stories had been shared during those times of exchange. The mysterious New World, the fantastically foreign West African spiritualities and their own Puritanical hysteria mixed with folklore and superstitions, were a powder keg of tension that created some of our earliest witchlore as an early country. Witchcraft is a staple of folklore in the colonies, especially the Middle colonies like Pennsylvania, a place where German-American folk magic was born from the folk magical practices of German immigrants. *Braucherie* (healers) and *hexerei* (witches) haunted the occult Christian mind of these immigrants during the Colonial era. Their practices precipitated a good deal of our general witchlore from that region.[27] Witchcraft fears in New York and New Jersey were as prevalent as they were in the New England and Southern colonies, shaped by the occult superstitions and Christian-hysteria of the Western European immigrants flooding into the New World.

The witch of New England - particularly of Massachusetts, Rhode Island and Connecticut, from the beginning was known and feared as a diabolic being with powers of foreknowledge and in congress with familiars who do their bidding. They weren't like the local conjure-woman who told fortunes and eased babies into the world, nor were they like the cunning folk who provided valuable services[28] (especially against evils). This was, of course, exasperated by the romanticisation of black conjure practices in late 18th century literature. Despite the embellishments of outsiders, the practice was very real, very strong at the time, and almost always associated with the magical work of blacks and "*mulattos*" in the area. Between the 16th and early 20th century, the conflation between cunning, conjure and craft was prevalent, and so much of what we gather from folklore is colored by these misunderstandings.

Witches could be the wild women, men and spirits who haunted woods and meadows, who danced with the Devil at midnight sabbats and would set their familiars on you, and unfortunately for the cunning folk, diviners, conjurors and fortune-tellers alike - all were condemned for their ways as witches none-the-less. They could also be afflicted individuals who were cursed by birth or misfortune with a penchant for natural evil-doing and magical workings.

Many African religious ideas also survived because they remained functional; indeed, white New Englanders as well as blacks visited black mediums and diviners, both feared the power of ghosts, witches, and conjurers, and both believed in the efficacy of herbal medicine and carried protective fetish charms for good luck. This, while it might seem surprising given the general perception of Yankee folklife, the folk traditions white New England met and blended with those of Africa to reinforce one another in a new Yankee folklore - a folklore that may have looked Euro-American, but was instead a complex, intercontinental alloy. (Piersen, 1988, p.86)[29]

Superstitions of witchcraft in New England reflected how different European peoples perceived the mystical world around them. The Northeast, being primarily influenced by Western European folk magical beliefs and those of the local West African population reflects the mentalities of the settlers and in the colonies. Witchcraft in New England has a famous history despite only being one place among many where witchcraft was a legal offence,[30] and that history isn't all white Puritan hysteria; it's also a history of the survival of the medicinal and divinatory traditions of black and mixed Americans. There is a history of People of Color in New England practicing the conjuring arts and other forms of folk magic for commerce and entertainment. The introduction of European folk magical customs into African folk magical practice was a result of observation on the slaves' part, and likewise, whites in the South and Northeast became familiarized with African magical practices through observation and interaction with their slaves[31] - and later, with their newly freed neighbors.

Street-side soothsayers, fortune tellers and diviners in Rhode Island, Vermont, Massachusetts and New York were more often than not referenced as black, black-Indigenous or *"mulatto"* folk magicians - *not witches*, who peddled in various magic including black arts and thus earned reputations for witchcraft involvement - accusations of which were not uncommon. The tradition of multiracial people being taught the magical practices of their ancestral lines is well documented as is the association of mixed people with witchcraft accusations,[32] and I don't mean famous figures like Tituba and Marie Laveau and their mythos and mystique.

Miscegenation, though illegal for a good part of American history, was not at all uncommon in the Northeast, Southeast or South. There are entire communities and ethnic groups defined by multiracial people in our country's history, with their own classifications and sense of culture; creoles, *mestizos*, "freed people of color", Black-Seminoles, etc. We are not a new novelty; we are American history. Slaves were often the victims of their master's lust; New Orleans even hosted *"quadroon balls"* to help wealthy white men find suitable multiracial sex slaves. Conversely, interracial coupling between blacks and whites, blacks and Natives and whites and Natives was not uncommon, nor were consenting marriages between the people. It would not have been uncommon for the children of white and black, or black and Native couples to absorb the folk medicine, magic and tales of both sides of their families, and it is evident that mixed people born on the East Coast and South contributed greatly to the syncretism we see between folk magical practices today.

Fortune-tellers along the East Coast were often these "in-betweeners" in a societal, racial and spiritual sense; referred to in our history by many pejorative designations, usually denoting their racial ambiguity. Despite the distrust of this new classification of "colored" people and their frequent involvement with fringe occupations including conjure and divination work, New Englanders of all kinds were happy to engage in magic when it suited them throughout the 18th, 19th and early 20th centuries, including acts we would call *witchcraft*. By the late 19th century, the thin racial barrier between folk magics had been pierced, and all but dissolved as more white Americans were involved in the practice of conjure and rootwork while African Americans had absorbed a good deal of German and English folk magical practices into their own; horseshoes and magical squares, pillow-magic and butter-churn magic had by then been absorbed into Afro-American folk magical work.

The combination of West African and Western European beliefs helped to precipitate the home-grown traditions of folk magic of the Northeast we know today. The Northeast, being a largely Protestant colonial area, served the survival of West African religious traditions less than Catholicism did in the South; without the saints and rituals of Catholicism to hide behind, slaves in the Northeast did not have the same level of protection offered by the religious parallels between West African religious structure and the Catholic religious structure.

New England is home to a good deal of European populations aside from English, Irish, French and German, and the folk magical practices of those people including Italians, Romani, Portuguese, Armenian and Jewish people are ingrained into the local lore of the old colonies. Their superstitions surrounding funeral customs, divination, ghosts and witches has shaped much of our collective culture's notions on witches. These days, witches of all kinds in this region celebrate their witch-trial heritage. They celebrate their Jewish, Italian, Irish, Portuguese, German, Dutch, English, French, Scandinavian and Spanish heritages by tapping into the traditions of folklore their ancestors brought to the Americas and making them their own - a distinctly American thing to do; and for those who are of mixed descent, the blending of similar traditions and paralleled folklore offers an opportunity to knit together the pieces of our identity into a cohesive fabric.

South, Southeast

The South is a rich hot bed of culture and cultural tension. It is the birthplace of our most famous magical traditions and is also the richest source of folklore regarding the pan-cultural perception of witchcraft itself. Many Americans across the country are a generation or two away from their Southern heritage, and for some of us that connection is strong. I grew up with an incredible plethora of hoodoo folklore from Florida on the side of my paternal black-Seminole relatives and it taught me a good deal about how much magic is part of the American cultural identity across the board. Southeastern indigenous people like the Seminoles played a deep role in the lives and developing diasporic religious traditions of African American slaves and their descendants as evidenced in the many paralleled and borrowed folklore and folktales between the two groups. My family may see themselves as Christian, but the hoodoo roots in their everyday lives were bare to the world. That familial experience also taught me that different people perceive things like "magic" and "witchcraft" and "evil" and "devil" in entirely different ways. Witches, while always dangerous, were also complex and easily conflated with the other magical folk out there.

Much of what white settlers perceived as *witchcraft* was simply the religious traditions of the different African tribes they had enslaved and Indigenous they had displaced. To the Christians, these practitioners of animistic religions of their own people were in league with the Devil; their drums and songs and wild rituals representing an *otherness*. West Africans held their own, very similar beliefs regarding people who could use magical forces for evil. Witch hunts were reported in West Africa in places like Ghana and surrounding areas where "witch-hunters" were an actual class of spiritual specialist.[33] There is magic in the West African traditional religions, including the magic of witches, but religious traditions of the Americas like New Orleans Voodoo are not witchcraft. Hoodoo, conjure, rootwork - none of these are inherently witchcraft traditions, though throughout history conjuremen and hoodoo women alike have met the same accusations of witchcraft. Witchcraft is an acknowledged practice by the standards of conjure, and conjurors themselves have been reported to, or even admitted to, practicing witchcraft even to the point of spiritual pact with the "Devil".

The magic of the Appalachians and Ozarks is what most people commonly associate with folk magic of the South outside of New Orleans Voodoo, but there are others; there are folk magical traditions throughout the South from the tip of Florida and all the way up North that would be insular to a family or a community. African American folklorist Zora Neal Hurston was reportedly initiated into several of these insular conjure traditions during her line of work, as was white folklorist Niles Newbell Puckett. Then, there are traditions of magic throughout the South that has publicly peddled charms and divinations and the lore that goes with it as a matter of everyday folk life. This includes the spells and conjurings of witchcraft too.

The various folk magical traditions that exist in America

today, especially in the South, are *deeply* syncretic, blending the Indigenous folk medicine of the Americas with African agrarian knowledge and animistic practices, with European folk magic and superstition (among other contributions). These traditions of the South are deeply tied to post-diaspora West African spirituality, just as the magic of the Southwest is deeply tied to Spanish folk-Catholicism and the Midwest's folk magic is deeply tied to German Christian folk practices. The syncretic religious systems of the Southeast and South are specifically rooted in Afro-Indigenous spiritual traditions, Catholic framework, Indigenous American medicine and various other bits and pieces. Arabic medicine in *Curanderismo*,[34] Chinese medicine featured in Cuban Santeria,[35] the influence of Filipino Catholicism in Louisiana Voodoo, or Basque, Jewish and African folk charms and remedies found in *brujeria* - it's amazing how spiritual beliefs and magical practices can shape and change people and their traditions over time.

Southwest

The Old World perceived witches as fearsome and terrible things capable of incredible evil; cannibals and conjurors who used diabolic materials and talismans to poison their victims, cast evil eyes, change shape and fly by spirit from their bodies. In the Southwest, witches were just as serious. Salem overshadowed the many witch trials and hangings that permeated the Southwest during the Western expansion era in American history.

Spanish Catholicism was ripe with superstition regarding witches and this was shared by the tribes of the Southwest, some of whom viewed witches as malevolent forces to be killed mercilessly (a sentiment shared with the Hispano settlers) and others who viewed witches as dangerous people capable of doing great good or great evil.

Belief in witchcraft in manipulation of supernatural powers for evil purposes was practically universal among American Indians. Many rites and customs of black magic indulged in by inhabitants of the New World bore a striking resemblance to practices found in Europe, Africa, the South Seas and elsewhere, for in whatever tribe or environment the craft appeared, there could be found the common belief that blame for human suffering often rested upon deliberate misuse of otherworldly powers by persons versed in the black arts. (Simmons, 1980, p.69)[36]

Witchcraft in the Southwest takes on many forms today. *Brujeria* is a popular manifestation of Mexican American and Afro-Latino spiritualities in the Southwest (among other places) and has come to represent practitioners of Latin American folk magic whether they are morally "good" or "bad". The fact is, most practitioners in the Southwest are Americans who were influenced by the folk magical beliefs of the Indigenous tribes around them, the folklore of Anglo Americans post-Spanish-American war and the Mexican American community that makes up a large swath of the populace in that region.

The folk magic here looks very different from that of New Orleans or from Salem. It will reflect the colors, scents and tastes of that region and the people who shaped it. Egg charms, *Milagros*, charms against *mal de ojo*, the recitation of certain prayers, the scent of sage, copal and sweet-grass, the use of turquoise and corn in protective charms - these are the folk magical practices you can find *here*, just as the South has her mojo bags and lucky rabbits' feet, the Midwest has its blessed medals and magic squares, the Northeast has its broom lore and poppets... Every region, shaped by the people, sharing in the traditions of magic.

Brujeria itself today is a fascinating social and political phenomenon; women and men of Latinx ancestry are tapping into the counterculture of witchcraft, the rebellion that it can inspire among youth to break with traditions. We've seen a rise of self-proclaimed *brujas* who have taken this once derogatory label and turned it into a matter of cultural expression, of joy in one's heritage. Much like the revitalization of conjure, rootwork and hoodoo among young African Americans, the rise of *brujas* in the Latin American community is offering people of color a chance at seeing themselves reflected in the world of witchcraft. We are moving away from eurocentricity in neo-paganism which has shaped so much of our occult media and into a place of representation.

A Crossroads of Cultures

The longer we gather folklore of North America, the more we see the endless connections between cultural and religious perspectives, and yet the whole study is ripe with contradiction and hypocrisy. The sheer fluidity and transformation as you move through the regions of the Americas is fascinating, but the similarities are the *real* show.

The prevailing perspective of the witch throughout American history was shaped by; the Church, print publications and rural folklore. Traditional North American witches have the unique opportunity to dissect and detangle the mixed-up history of witchlore, to cultivate practices recreated from those of our pre and post-colonial ancestors. From the folkloric collections of B.A Botkin, Frank C. Brown, Wayland D. Hand, the Tennessee Folklore Society, the *Journal of American Folklore*, Zora Neale Hurston, Hubert J. Davis and Niles Newbell Puckett among others, combined with the oral traditions, story-telling and general superstitions around us, we are able to extract some idea of what was once common beliefs of the folk - of our African American, European and Indigenous American ancestors as they interacted on this spiritual level.

American folk magic and witchcraft is a crossroads of clashing cultures. Brought together by adversity, theft, enslavement, expansion, love, war and liberty, our culture as Americans is defined by our diversity, and our traditions of magic was birthed first by a synthesis of European, African and Indigenous spiritual beliefs and superstitions, and then later by all the many parts of the world.

The spirit of the *crossroads* is a cross-cultural concept that permeated witchlore. In the States, the crossroads is the spiritual platform of the Witchking and the Hags of night It is the meeting place of sabbats and the sacred place where offerings are left. Like the compass, the crossroads is symbolic of the ways that come together, the worlds that intersect, the directions, the elements, the winds and the divisions of the powers. At these places where the worlds meet, our ancestors of various cultures held deeply rooted superstitious fear - the power of these places to instruct or ensnare was a risk many were unwilling to dare. This liminal place, associated with psychopomps like Hekate and Exú, is the bridge that shows the spirit roads and those roads witches travel. It is the sacred nexus where powers and ideas meet and the path that separates worlds becomes intangible. We witches pass through this membrane to worlds unseen and return again to our bodies, in dream or nightmare.

As an American, the crossroads can symbolize the intersection of peoples and times; the many ways by which the winds blow, the directions of this land, the elements that surround us, even the medicine wheel. The place between worlds, this is a sacred space we can find anywhere around us if we look correctly. Here, at these places of intersecting pathways, witches are meant to leave offerings to the spirits, or the Devil's due, and to never, ever look back. Those old gods who dwell in these places are always associated with witchcraft and magic.

The definition of a witch and who was accused of being such changes depending on the time and who you ask, but in the States and North America itself, the witch was the symbolic synthesis of all the world's greatest occult fears combined into the motif we know today; the night-flying, cunning creature who haunts woods and dreams, who tricks and heals as they please.

Each culture's misunderstandings of one another only served to reinforce their beliefs in witches and other magical creatures. Witchcraft was supposed to have been a dark art but then again, shamans, cunning folk, magicians, folk-healers - every kind of practitioner has been accused of evil acts by association with witchery, and even still, plenty of witches have been known to be "good" or beneficial beings. With such a nebulous definition of witchcraft, we're bound to have deep disagreements with one another, but that's alright. The crossroads is a place for things to meet, even opposing ideas and cultural perceptions; I say we meet there in that middle ground to celebrate our differences and our similarities.

Chapter 4

Witch Blood

By Sin and Silver Bullets

They say some witches are born, not initiated. You may spy them by their strange differences; if they have red hair, or were a seventh daughter born on Christmas,[37] or if they were born with a caul over them. Some persons are born as witches because it is simply the way they are. The naturally born witch had a certain *something* about them that marked them so; even a literal mark could give it away. Witchcraft itself does not require an initiation ritual *per se,* but there is a good deal of wisdom to be learned from the witchcraft initiation mythos that surround our folklore. From the tales of witch-making, we learn about how fear is transmitted between people, how traditions of folklore are passed between groups, and how magical actions transcend cultural boundaries. The initiatory process is symbolic of death and rebirth - an action that is part of many religious rites-of-passage. These acts of death and rebirth happen in a number of fashions, some a little stranger than others.

They say some people are born half in this world and half out. It's an old trope, one promoted more so as neo-paganism has grown. The idea of a witch being someone set-apart by some naturally otherworldly aspect or as a person in-tune with the spiritual world is an old one, and remains popular today. To be born or gifted (or cursed, depending on how you look at it) with the ability to move between the worlds, to fly by spirit, to be served by familiars and devils, this was indicative of a witch, and there was a good deal of legend and lore regarding these people. Were they the spawn of evil? Were they the product of angels and demons copulating with humans? Our ancestors weren't quite sure, so they developed an array of stories and tales just to explain why some people seemed to have an inclination for the strange and occult. We haven't gotten much closer to answering these questions today. In these modern times, witchcraft is a lot more nebulous and interpretive; much of the mystique has been replaced by a more practical and symbolic interpretation of magic, but not for everyone. There are still many places in this world, in this country, that truly believes that witches are a not-altogether-human force of nature or evil that still haunts our nightmares.

In the Southwest where I was born, a natural or birth witch was marked by the presence of an *"evil eye"* - something in the darkness or the strangeness of those eyes that showed a devil lurking behind them. Perhaps the child was born with a long tooth or two - this could mark a witch! Young girls, more often than most others, were susceptible to being witches; an art they learned through selling their bodies to the Devil, by working for a familiar, or could even learn the craft through their mothers.[38] Like America itself, the method by which one becomes a witch is diverse and varied and shaped by the people who surround them and the region in which they are living.

There're a hundred different versions of the tale of how a witch comes to be. Sometimes he sells his soul for power, sometimes he's born gifted with power; sometimes he barters with the Devil, sometimes with fairies or spirits of all kinds; sometimes becoming a witch is a curse placed on you, sometimes it's a curse you bring upon yourself; some people are said to be witches without even knowing it! Some witches are made by tying a knot in a willow tree, renouncing their baptism and embracing the "devil".[39] Some German-American folklore suggests that all that is needed is for you to be pointed at or spoken to by a witch and you could become one.

Witchcraft as an involuntary result of one's very spirit is seen primarily in African American conjure lore,[40] which sometimes viewed conjurors as those with mastery over mysterious arts and witches as a person born with innate abilities to cause the harm conjurors were paid to perform. The *Journal of American Folklore* and the folklore of North Carolina have a lot to say about how witches become witches; by shooting silver bullets or scouring pewter or tin plates.[41] A few German-Judaic stories collected in Pennsylvania describe witches not as a *person*, but as an entity which can become caught in your own clothes as you wear them[42] - more like a class of *spirit* than human initiate. A witch could be an affliction, this is true. Even in New Mexico folklore a witch could be a malady afflicted upon some poor soul; *"The unfortunate individual who is beset by witches is also pursued and molested by devils and other evil spirits who help the witches."* (Green, p.166)[43]

How one becomes a witch seems to depend entirely on the situation, from the perspective of the cultures who disseminated these superstitions, but what all of the folklore has taught is that there are many paths to the craft, and none of them should be taken lightly. In Colonial era witchlore, the witch needs only to take their oath of service to whatever is granting their power, or whatever it is they hold faith in, and then get to work. It really is that simple, which is why witches belong to all kinds of cultures and religions; witchcraft is an action that defines you, and you get to define those actions and yourself along with it. After all, it is the mystic art of the layperson and any person is capable of witching whether they know it or not - the trick is *believing*.

Again, it is the process of death and rebirth that is most symbolic and important to the idea of initiation ritual - if an initiation ritual is sought. In regards to Colonial witchlore, often, the witch had already been baptized at birth as a Christian and then later underwent confirmation as was commonplace for Catholics and Christians, and so the additional step of *"washing the grace away"* by ablution in water while renouncing your allegiance to your former religion was important - a way to distance your soul from the old oath made to that god.

Washing away the old to usher in the new is one of those old witching superstitions that universally appeals; the idea of making a formal declaration between you and the spirit world by symbolic and literal purification of the self. You'll see this often in North American folktales of witches; initiation through removal of clothes, old oaths, morals, even virginities. Shedding the old and becoming reborn, the symbolism is deeply entrenched and because of this, valuable to understand. Initiation may not be necessary to the practice of witchcraft, but it is a powerful line of tradition found throughout our shared magical practices that should not be lost.

The Witch's Many Options

Those who want to become witches go forth at night to the Sabbat, and there they perform three somersaults, but first they call upon the devil, to whom they all give themselves; they renounce their faith in god three times, and then spit into their hands; after they have rubbed their hands together three times, they are carried off by the devil in spirit, and leave the body behind bloodless and dead, until the devil returns the spirit to it. (Ginzburg, 1966, p.95) [44]

The witch is spoiled for choice where initiatory options are concerned. Initiations didn't always have to be a lonely affair at some hilltop; in fact, initiations were often a social event in our folklore. A witch can initiate another through a manner of formal schooling, or, could be done through sexual congress with an initiated witch of the opposite sex. Other times it's the same traditional sabbatic initiation of English lore, and other times, it's a strange incident altogether that creates the witch - a happenstance like wandering into the midst of a sabbat and being taken for a night-ride. It depends on the cultural perspective; Thomas A. Green reported in *Latino American Folktales* (2009) that *"No one is born a witch. Witchcraft is a science, a kind of learning which may be learned from other witches. Near Pena Blanca, in central*

New Mexico, here is said to be a school of witches."[45] Following an aspirant's arrival at the supposed school of witches, they would be taught shape-shifting and other magics and could either be given their powers from another witch, or, could pact with the Devil for power.

In Kentucky and Tennessee superstition, a witch can be made numerous ways, including just by asking the Devil nine times or calling to him on the road. Nine is an important piece of this folk-narrative; the devil must be prayed to nine times at a crossroads or on a hilltop. Also, a witch can be made by a shooting a silver bullet and killed by being shot by one; she can be made by the Devil but saved by God. In Nova Scotia and New York anti-witch charms, shooting the picture of a witch with a silver bullet or silver fragments was supposed to make the witch fall down dead! Just as silver is the method to kill, it is also a symbol of a witches' initiation according to lore just a few States away.

A Kentucky folktale, *The Red Rag Under the Churn*[46] highlights a number of witchlore motifs; the knotted cord, the butter-churn witch, initiation by the Devil and his court of witches, familiar spirits and the Devil's book. The combination of these witch-initiation motifs underscores how prevalent these ideas were among the common people's oral traditions and folk magical fears, whether they were fears, fables or folklore.

In eastern Kentucky, one who desires to become a witch goes before sunrise to the summit of an adjacent mountain. As soon as the sun begins to appear above the distant horizon, and as soon as the aspirant as hurled a trine anathema at Jehovah, and owned the Devil as a master, she holds up a white handkerchief in front of it, shoots through the 'kerchief with a silver bullet, and blood drops from it. The operation is then complete. (Journal of American Folklore, 1914, p.329)

A similar formula from a second source, *American Folk Tales and*

Songs: Jack and the Witches by Richard Chase, tells the same tale of the Devil's mountain and the white cloth, but this time, animal sacrifice is added;

> *...and the Devil took her in: told her, like he done the others, all about how to be a witch - boillin' a black cat at sun-up on the east side of a mountain to get the witch bone shootin' at the sun with a silver bullet, and washin' your hands in a spring nine times with strong lye soap and sayin every time you rinse,*
> *"I wish my soul as free from grace,*
> *as my two hands are free of grease!"*[47]

Cloth, like a handkerchief, is a recurrent theme in the South, especially knot lore. According to some folklore of the Appalachians, a witch could be made by going to a spring with a sponsor witch and being anointed in the water while knotting three corners of the handkerchief (but not the last), while denouncing the trinity. After a short ritual twirl the Devil would appear with his iron pen and black book to take her name.[48] Knots, and water are common threads in Southern witchlore. The importance of cleaning an object and dedicating oneself to the Devil through the purification of water is elsewhere found in sources of the South;

> *Among the mountain whites of the southern Alleghenies it was possible some twenty years since for a man to acquire forbidden knowledge by scouring a tin or pewter plate in some secret place, and giving himself to the Devil by saying, "I will be as clean of Jesus Christ as this dish is of dirt".*(Cross, p.17)[49]

A mountain, at sunrise, is a running theme in Southern and Midwestern witchlore, and as always, the Pact between the seeker and the spirit is present. This method of the Devil or a witch placing a hand on the head and one on the foot and declaring 'all between it to belong to the Devil' is referenced in Western European witch trial lore quite a bit, and found its way into the general folklore of the Americas:

> To become a witch, the candidate goes with the Devil to the top of the highest hill at sunrise nine successive days and curses God. The Devil then places one hand on the candidate's head and one on his feet, and receives the promise that all between his hands shall be devoted to his services. (FCB, p.110)[50]

Cultural motifs and folk narrative play a large part in how we develop and disseminate folklore and one of the most fascinating narratives of New World witchlore is the Pact between witch and devil. It's a pretty standard model from the European witch-hunts; the witch is to strip nude, renounce former religion, sign their name in the book of the beast and agree to do the Devil's bidding in exchange for power. There can be additional steps such as acts of profaning against the bible or performing the supposed *Osculum Infame* (kissing the Devil's butt) - or there could be significantly less steps; a simple renouncement and a spiritual offer. This narrative is particularly important to the foundation of how Christianized people in the New World conceptualized witchcraft and how those influences continue in our media and culture.

African American folklore storytelling, which is of course one of the more important facets of folkloric transmission, has some fun witchlore, inspiring to the imagination. One tale, *The Ways of a Witch* as told by William J. Faulkner in *Talk That Talk: An Anthology of African American Storytelling*[51] is a fascinating example of the witch-initiation narrative involving a spiritual Pact; in this story, a woman is to find a hollow stump in the woods full of water, this woman is to go down to a cornfield and find an ear of multi colored "Indian corn" and every Friday leave a kernel on the stump. Eventually, a jaybird is to come and deliver one of the offerings to the Devil himself, who, after seven weeks, will appear to make a deal with the witch.

In the Southwest, things differed greatly from people to people; some tribes like the Navajo had complicated relationships with witchcraft, while some Pueblo tribes believed that anyone could be a witch if they were sad, angry, hurt or marginalized enough, and still, others saw witchcraft more like an employment opportunity which could elevate fame and status but wasn't tied to a specific evil. In the Northwest, witches weren't ones to make oaths to an entity like a devil or demon - they *became* great good or great evil depending on who they were. They served the same spirits personified in nature that the community did; they simply used the *medicine* for evil rather than good; locally, a witch could be identified by their connection or use of owl, snake or snail medicine - all of these entities being familiars of death and associated with calamity and dark work.

There seems to be a good deal of disagreement on the matter, and there does appear to be a great many ways that one may actively or passively become a practitioner of magic; witchcraft in particular. Of the folklore I've studied, what initiation into witchery often boils down to are some simple components in the European model: The **calling**, the **acceptance**, the **contract** and the **gift**. We see versions of this in the wood prints of the witch-trial era; witches being sought by the Devil, wooed by him, desecrating the bible, renouncing their faith, signing their name, dancing with the Devil and obtaining their familiar. It's an all-too-common motif that has permeated our imaginations since before the Colonial days. There were steps to be taken in terms of the initiatory process with a devil/spirit and it all came down to some fundamental components:

Calling by the spirits: in most regards, the craft is initiatory - even when the initiation is brought about in private by the spirits. Common folklore provides examples of callings in the forms of visitations from the spirits in dreams or in person, or, being spirited away (like *Jack and the Witches* of Southern lore), or, the sudden revelation of power. This may be a holdover from the time of the witch trial records, but it has since joined the broader folklore of witchcraft. *What* calls the witch varies from place to place, person to person, culture to culture: in many cases a witch is called by her own ambitions and desires, in other cases he is called by the spirits or demons or wee-folk without much of a choice. The calling is a very personal thing, but once it is heard, it is the first step in pursuing witchcraft.

Acceptance, or, the renunciation of old oaths: acceptance of the terms and conditions set forth by whatever spirits or gods or coven has called you to the craft. In order to accept the terms of the spirits, traditionally one would then be expected to renounce all former allegiances (washing away the grace, saying the lord's prayer backwards, the like). After one has rid themselves of old oaths, they are free to promise their soul elsewhere - to spirits, devils, demons or gods.

Contract, or oath to the spirits/gods": a contract of give-and-take between you and whatever entity has called to you. In folklore, there is a distinct understanding that whoever takes up witchcraft is doing so with the aid of unseen allies and familiars, and these entities have their own demands for the power they give; whether it is to suckle from the witch's teat or be fed of butter and cream. The contract with the Devil takes the shape of a ritual at sunrise or the signing of one's name in his book or some other symbolic action of dedication. A contract with a coven may call for a sexual union or a blood price - some kind of congress as a form of initiation. This feature of the practice is a holdover of superstitions from the Witch Trial era of the Old World and New, but it has found its way into the traditional practices of modern witches across the world.

When a woman decides to become a witch, according to the fireside legends she repairs to the family buryin' ground at midnight, in the dark of the moon. Beginning with a verbal renunciation of the Christian religion, she swears to give herself body and soul to the Devil. She removes every stitch of clothing, which she hangs on an infidel's tombstone, and delivers her body immediately to the Devil's representative - that is, to the man who is inducting her into the "mystery." (Randolph, 1947, p.267)[52]

A contract with the spirits can look very different; no book perhaps and no orgiastic rite maybe, but there are specific expectations one may be expected to live up to in terms of Sacrifice and Service. When one makes a deal with the otherworldly, one is agreeing to otherworldly terms in exchange for the *delicious* gifts they bestow upon the seeker, and this often takes the form of an oath or specific ritual or taboo that must be observed.

Gift, or, obtainment of a familiar or ally, or, of one's symbolic or literal source of power. This *familiar spirit* often took the form in lore as some kind of spirit or imp or animal, or could be an object; a witch-bone, root, lodestone or some other talisman or amulet of power. This symbol, personification, object, entity or talisman serves as a source and a conduit. Whether material or incorporeal, whatever gift is being given here, it must be honored and protected, otherwise true harm could come to the witch - as is the case for a witch whose witch-bone goes missing, or whose lodestone goes unfed. The witch will wither, the witch will die, if they do not honor their gift.

A few methods of initiation that may appeal to the modern folkloric witch in the New World have Old World origins and elements deeply embedded into early American perceptions of the spiritual initiation. When pursuing the modern adaption of these old school rituals, we will improve and reinvent in our own individual ways; witches have the liberty to be fluid and evolved and progressive as a spirituality while still holding true to the traditional narratives and foundations that we so love. This is most true here in the New World, where all that we have is a cross-cultural culmination of spiritual experiences which have forged the general lore of our regions, our people, our country.

Depending on who you are and where you come from, the method by which you undergo the traditional initiatory process may vary. Perhaps you are schooled, perhaps you are born initiated, or maybe you were cursed... but for most, the process of dedication is part of the tradition of witch-crafting that cannot be overlooked, a means by which we connect through the common rite-of-passage. Speaking of foundations and traditions, what are some common initiation symbols to keep in mind when moving forward in this part of the craft?

- Hours of sunrise, sunset or midnight - these liminal hours being frequently part of the initiation lore of the South, Northeast, Southwest and Midwest.
- Days of folkloric importance to the sabbatic flight and ecstatic celebrations of witches include **Hallows Eve, May's Eve** (Easter, Beltane, Walpurgisnacht), **Midsummer** (St. Johns - Solstice), **Midwinter** (Christmas, Yule) and **New Year's Eve.** Usually, **Fridays** and **Tuesdays** are believed to be the days that witches use to do their tricks and charms while Wednesdays and Sundays were ill-luck to a witch. The numbers **three, seven** and **nine** play a prominent role in the repetition of actions recommended for summoning the Black Man at the Crossroads.
- Places of importance for witching work tend to be liminal spaces; the local woods, a mountainside, hillside, meadow, a graveyard, river or some sacred natural space known locally of importance, such as a known haunt, ruins or a

spring. A wagon road is referenced in the Brown collection; one is to make a circle there and call the Devil to *"take me ring and all!"*[53] The woods are a sacred place; it's where the ferns that witches dance around on St. John's Eve are found, it's where we're said to be found riding to sabbats. In Virginian folklore, it was believed that when a person became a witch in their family, they would be expected to leave the house and live in the wild wood or a cave.[54]

- One could tie a petition-knot to a sacred witching tree (such as an elder, blackthorn or willow), renounce their old ties and offer themselves to the spirit or entity that called to them.

- Or, go to a crossroads, make a circle, leave an offering, renounce your former ties and offer yourself to the cross-roads spirit who meets you there. The spirit of the crossroads in the Americas usually wears black (as opposed to the man-in-green sometimes seen at crossroads in the Old World) and they can take many forms, and have many names. To some he is a folk devil, to others, the Devil of the bible. To some he is a musician of great skill who teaches the best, to others he is the trickster spider Aunt Nancy, or perhaps a tall-hatted man in black, or maybe at the crossroads awaits the Witchqueen, or fairy queen, wailing woman or Hag riding the night. *To this witch, the witch-masters are the Horned One of the Wood and the Hag of Winter. *

- Another, and far easier traditional initiation calls for the seeker to stand with one hand over their head and one over their foot declaring all between it to belong to whatever spirit has called them (or whatever it is the witch will serve if they serve at all). The same could be done by kneeling on the ground with your hands on the ground on either side of you declaring all between them to belong to the Devil, etc. Or, as I like to say with my hands touching two parallel trees whose roots meet beneath my feet, *"All that stands between these hands, serves the spirits and these lands."*

A calling to witchcraft, acceptance of yourself as one, an oath of service to your spirits, a contract that binds you and the many gifts you receive are all it can take, and there are definitely ways to adapt the models of some of the old lore to fit our modern needs. Other methods of initiation worthy of note for their frequency of appearance in lore include the obtainment of an object which grants witching; such as a root, a witch-bone or a lodestone. Even the eating of *grasshoppers* and *crickets* could turn a person into a witch according to the Brown collection.

The truth is, witchcraft is an action, it is a way one lives their lives and it doesn't really matter if your converted or were born with it. Witches don't belong to some specific bloodline, there is no witch-gene, we are not all descended from angels or fairies. Some people find it as teenagers, some have it find them when they're adults. Some people are inspired by movies and shows, and some, like me, grew up so spiritually broad that witchcraft was just the natural progression. It doesn't matter if it runs in your family or if you first heard about it in a comic book - if you delve and dabble enough in it, it will become what you are.

Skeletal Initiations: The Witch Bone

Black Cat Witch Bones, Moles Paw, Toad Bones and Rabbit's Feet

A bit of initiation power associated with early Afro-Caribbean conjure storytelling and English folklore which made its way into North and South Carolinian lore, is the creation of a witch through the obtaining of a "witch-bone" which is supposed to provide a witch with his status and power once properly taken. Sometimes, obtaining the witch-bone involved boiling the cat and tossing the bones in a river, or simply picking a bone from the boiling pot, or even passing the bones through your mouth in front of a mirror.[55]

> *Amulets of animal bone appear to be both ancient and worldwide. The magical power of the black **cat bone** and its associated rituals have been documented, in nearly identical forms, in Hungary, Finland, and Ireland, as well as countries colonized by Europeans, including the United States, Canada, the Philippines, and the Cape Verde Islands. The English "Toadmen" tradition is strikingly parallel. When the proper bone from a toad is recovered through rituals very similar to those of the black cat, its owner acquires a variety of uncanny powers, including the ability to become invisible, cure various ailments, and attract good fortune.* (Prahlad, 2016, p.31)[56]

There were a few ways you could become a witch by obtaining a specific animal's bone according to folklore, and none of it was a kind experience for the animal involved. If one wanted to become a witch or a magician with the powers of conversation, divination, eloquence, healing and legal acumen, one was advised by Pliny and Agrippa to smother a mole. If one desired to have the power to speak with horses or to change skins, they could stake a toad (a distinctly English tradition and passed into small pockets of American folklore). Or, if one decided to wield the power of luck, wealth and protection from evil, they may be advised by a conjurer to cut the hind foot off of a graveyard rabbit...

But, if a person wanted to immediately come into a good deal of initiatory power, luck, flight, invisibility, and more, the most classic of Southern folkloric witch-bone charms is that of the boiled black-cat bone. Moles, toads, rabbits and cats, much like snakes, owls and frogs, are well known familiar spirits to witches, a sentiment shared by early Americans of all kinds, and cats were by far the most cunning creature.

> *To become a witch, drop a live black cat into a black kettle of boiling water. (If I remember correctly, the time specified was midnight). When the flesh has separated from the bones, collect all the bones, take them to the river, and drop them in. No matter how swift the water is, one of the bones will rise and float up the stream. This is the witch-bone, and as long as you keep it, you are a witch.* (FCB, p.113)

Animal symbolism, sacrifice and familiarity are standards across the board in American witchery, even though we modern witches will find most of these operations sickening to attempt. Sacrifice is one of the most prominent aspects of magical practice, and our ancestors had some pretty curious notions on the nature of sacrifice and magic:

> *Zora Neale Hurston,* In Mules and Men: Negro Folktales and Voodoo Practice in the South *(1935), explains the importance of the black cat bones in hoodoo and describes a ceremony for selecting the correct bone by boiling the cat and passing the bones through her mouth until one tasted bitter (221). Puckett describes a similar ceremony where the person should pass the bones through the mouth while looking into a mirror.* (Sanders, 2003, p.70)[57]

What we can take away from the violent and sacrificial initiation stories are information on the ritualism and symbolism behind the birth of a witch. These superstitions were bloodthirsty and sacrificial, feeding old, hungry, merciless spirits of a world far more mysterious and fearful than our own.

Sacrificial attitudes aside, the idea of a witch-bone is an important one. While we can interpret the folklore literally regarding a black-cat, the concept is actually a lot more diverse than that. A "witch-bone" or talisman which bestows magical power or symbolizes the Pact, could be a sacred root kept and fed, or a lodestone which would be fed lest it kill its owner. More so, a witch-bone is the seat of power within someone. Whether or not you believe in the cosmology of witch-blood and the divine heritage of the sorcerer, what is true is that the *Will* of a practitioner is a special thing, and it comes from a place within us that acts as the vinculum between us and that otherworldly god-well of power.

Or, maybe the witch-bone is even more metaphorical than all that, representing our sheer will-power and the "spirit" of the witch. From a practical standpoint, a symbol of one's pact in the form of a talisman or object of power is an old tradition and one that ought not to be lost as we modernize. For some of us, the connection was an unavoidable part of our initiation into the craft, this object which feeds us as we feed it. Sometimes a root, sometimes a stone, and sometimes a bone.

One way to implement the witch-bone tradition in a non-literal sense is to obtain an object of power by chance rather than by seizing the power. While the whole point of the witch-bone tradition as with toadmen and mole-magicians, is to take the part from the animal while it is still living (the idea being that a living animal's life force will concentrate in that piece you've taken after you've killed it). I'd argue that what this really represents is the necessary ordeal or trial that needs to take place in order for someone to obtain power. Power should never come easy; it always has some kind of price and this price serves a purpose.

I stand against the abuse of animals presented in this lore, and so my personal recommendation would be to seek out a root (which also requires you to kill an entire plant as the root is sort of necessary for its survival, make of that what you will morally) or find a loadstone, or seek out a "witch-bone" in the more symbolic magical sense, because it really doesn't matter what symbol or object (if any) symbolizes your relationship with the craft, what matters is that *you* know your own source of power. The point of this kind of magic is to form a relationship with an object that has its own spirit, its own gifts to offer, and sharing in that power. This connection is one prized in witch fables across the world, across history; the importance of an ally for a witch cannot be ignored, especially those allies which are forged through the exchange of power.

These relationships can be temperamental, you must never allow yourself to neglect your allies; whether a lodestone, *alraune* or witch bone, because an object of power is said to have a life of its own, and if you show no value to that life, it will show none to you. In many ways - most ways really, the craft is all about connection and creation.

Chapter 5

Tricks, Projects, Fortunes, and Charms

Three times throw oaken ashes in the air,
Three times sit still in an old armchair:
Three-times-three ties a true lover's knot,
And say he will, or he will not.
Go burn poison ivy in a hot blue fire,
With some screech owl feathers and a prickly briar,
Some cedar gathered at a dead man's grave,
And all your cares and fears an end will have.
- Thomas Campion, as told by Mrs. Maude Minish Sutton,
Lenoir, Caldwell county[58]

In the New World, we *lay **tricks*** rather than spells, our love
charms are ***projects***, our divinations are fortunes. The witches
perform all manner of conjure and craft. Their best days are
Tuesdays and Fridays, at sunset or midnight, in groves, graves or
grottos they lurk and do their crooked work. They serve the land
and the bones within it, they serve the sun, moon, and places
in-between. They dance with devils and fly-by-night. That is the
way of witches.

Charms of magic transcend religious boundaries and
permeate our imaginations and our faiths. The charms we know
today are most often hold-overs from those who came before us.
We can trace their worries and daily fears through their common
superstitions. We can view the world through their experiences
when we tap into the charms they too utilized. Magic like this is
an heirloom, one we ought to treasure for the simple lesson to
be learned. Some charms are silly and stupid, others are timeless
and meaningful. Some charms make sense, others do not, but
they do help frame the way magic was thought of throughout

history. Someday, the little magics we practice will be the folk charms of our children.

Charms, tricks, and tools of the trade are vast throughout the country. Some folk remedies and operations have been here so long, that we hardly know where they could have sprung from or who started their tradition. Other charms of the trade are well known for being rooted in the lore of a particular people. Generally, whatever comes to America and gets spread in talk or written word becomes the new normal, it becomes ingrained into our superstitions and sayings and as we are a nomadic group who move between our regions fluidly, we seed the folklore we've been fed in new places every day.

Witch bottles are a well-known facet of African American conjure magic in the South and yet the origin of these bottles is undoubtedly a European inspiration; mojo bags, medicine bags and magic bundles are now common to folk magic among white Americans but their origins lie in West African and Southeast Native American fetish and protective charms. Horseshoes and bloodroot were absorbed into African American folk magic just as various hoodoo and conjure skills were absorbed *out* of African American folk magic. The tools of magic we use have a long history of exchange and the common folk who interacted with one another every day, shared a deep wealth of information found paralleled between their cultures, and from this synthesis American Folk Magical Traditions were born.

Magic in the New World tended to follow some pretty specific laws whether the practice was witchery, cunning or conjure. **Sympathetic** magic and **Contagion** are two sides of the same coin; the idea that one could affect change by likeness or by connection is the basis for most folk magic itself, and **Triplicity** plays a strong part in this (repetitions of actions in threes is a long-standing process in magic that continues prominence in New World traditions). The process of ensouling or "Spirit-Embodiment" figures prominently in Afro-Diaspora and Latin magical traditions; the idea that a spirit could inhabit an object and be worshiped or served through that object remains a powerful practice; the act of directing the soul inside the object to serve the practitioner in some way speaks to the animistic heart of folk magic itself. Objects of all kinds could channel spiritual power; they could even become vessels of divine power with their own motives and desires. When we speak of magical tools, we are talking about the power that any object in the world can have over our lives, and the power we give to those materials.

To every material, there exists a potential power, a correspondence with the world around it that allows it to make a spiritual impact - at least that's the theory of magical tools; and these tools were as innumerable and diverse as the people who used them. The tools of hexing in Southwestern witchcraft may include dolls, lodestones, knots and image magic charms while the hexing tools of the Midwest may include things like hairballs (witch-bullets), black-bottles (witch-bottles) and railroad spikes. The tools of each area will reflect the primary populations who settled there; Southwestern witchcraft traditions are of Spanish, Indigenous and Anglo-American influences; the witchcraft traditions of New England are a blend of English, German, West African and Indigenous; the witchcraft traditions of the South will primarily reflect Irish, Indigenous American, African, Afro-Caribbean, and East Indian influences. These regions were shaped by all kinds of people and the folk magic there was shaped by the combined superstitions of these people as well.

Each region and the demographic of people that reside there had their own folklore - some unique, some common. Below is a general key of charms, tools, and superstitions commonly found in the collections of American folklore or in oral history. I've included a key to help you identify the region where you are most likely to find these charms and superstitions mentioned in folklore or in circulation today. They can be invaluable to understanding the history of magical works in our country and how it has moved and expanded with us.

Key: N, (North) NE (Northeast), S (South), SE (South East), SW (South West), NW (Northwest), MW (Midwest), CA (Canadian), AA (African American specifically), TA (Traditional American), G (General American)

Agrarian

-To Be Lucky
Gardening by moon phases (G), lucky clovers (G), lavender (G), roses (G)

-To Honor Harvest, Winter, Spring, and Summer:
Corn dolls, carved-pumpkins (G)
Yule logs and evergreen burnings (NE)
May crowns and baskets (NE, SE), decorated Easter eggs (G)
Sun wheels and fern seeds (NE, MW, G)

Anathemic

-To Hex an Enemy:
Witch bottle (NE, S, SE, SW)
Witch bullet (MW, NE, SE, S)
Witch bone (NE, MW, SE, S, SW)
Pillow Charms (MW, S, SE, AA, German-American)[59]
Red, white or black salt (G)
Red and black pepper (S, SE, MW, SW, G)
Yellow or black mustard seed (S, SE, MW, G)
Garlic sacks,[60] Onions hanging (MW, SW, G)
Pins, needles, nails, stakes (G), devil's club (NW)
Lodestone (S, SW), anvil dust (SE)
Living-Things-Within: lizards, spiders, snails, frogs, toads, salamanders, scorpions, snakes and worms (G)

-Protect from Bewitchment:

Silver bullets (G)

Quicksilver and tinfoil (AA, S, SE, G) silver amulets (G)

Animal charms, sacred prayer papers or magic squares (NE, MW, S, SE)

Payer books, rice, seeds, garlic sacks, onion sacks, pepper wreaths (S, SE, SW, G)

Gun incantations (MW)

Fairy-Crosses (S, SE)

Horseshoes hung over entrances (MW, G)

Witch-cakes (NE, TA - *a distinctly Salem Trial bit of folk-magic*)

Heart-shaped lockets or brooches to reproach the evil eye[61] (S)

Crushed eggs (S, SW) - - *in the South and Midwest, it was recommended that one crush eggshells used in the home or witches would sail them over the seas,[62] in the Southwest, deep South and Caribbean, crushed eggshells in the form of cascarilla have anti-evil eye properties and protective charm*).

-To Protect from Poison/Gossip:

Graveyard dirt (S), slippery elm (S)

Apotropaic

-To Avert Evil Eye:

Salt - Afro-American folklore details salt as one of the most important minerals to have on hand, especially when dealing with other practitioners, as salt was believed to prevent witches from crossing into places, returning to their bodies after night-riding.[63] English folklore had similar applications for salt; to banish witches, to swear oaths,[64] to appease fairies, to undo a curse or to bless homes according to Rosemary Guiley in *The Encyclopedia of Witches, Witchcraft & Wicca* (p.305): *"Sharing salt is symbolic of establishing a deep bond between people. When a new home was occupied, salt was often one of the first things to be brought across the threshold in order to drive away evil influences and establish good energy and luck."* Salt sprinkled in an errant lover's tracks could turn them back and salt sprinkled in a fire every day with a prayer or chant, the lover would return. They say witchcraft itself is repelled by salt, and that spirits and demons are driven away from it, and certainly cannot cross a line of salt. The salt superstitions are so ingrained into American folklore it is one of the more important items in a toolbox of traditional witchery.

-To Purify a Space or Person:
Saltwater (G), holy water, bathing on St. John's Eve (G)
Florida water (S)
Smudge smoke(G)

Auspicious
 -To Draw Luck/Wealth:
Horse tooth (S), gator tooth (S)
Silver coins (G), gold rings (G), penny (G)
Buckeye (S, SE)
Four-hole buttons (NE, SE)
Horseshoe (G)
Wishbone (G)
Lockets (S), broaches, figurines - *small objects of great personal power which bare some deep meaning to the keeper* (G)
Black cat bone (S, SE, MW)

-To Banish Ill Luck:
Four thieves' vinegar (S)
Silver coins (MW), silver bullets (MW, S SE), quicksilver and liquid mercury (S, common in Afro-American hoodoo and conjure-work),[65] forks and spoons (S, MW)

-To Bless a House:

Salt, bread, butter (G)
St. John's Wort collected on Midsummer's Eve, May Baskets and May Wreaths (NE, MW, G)

-*To Grow in Power of Speech and Mind*:
Mole (G)
Buckeye (S, MW)
Sugar (S), honey (S)

Divinatory

Portents of the dead, omens of things to come, oracles which determine the rights and wrongs of life; these were all shared facets of everyday life itself among the folk spirituality of German and English settlers, Hispano setters in the Southwest and the Pueblo they encountered there, among slaves from the Congo and Cameroon, among Chinese immigrants and East Indian merchants - it has always been believed that omens, signs, and symbols are all around us waiting to be interpreted and that we could alter the path of our lives by reading these fortunes and seeking what lies beyond. These kinds of beliefs are passed down in families and between friends and through story-telling.

These days you can find IChing, tarot, runes and palmistry kits in any given book store countertop across the country while in the past, common non-witch fortune-telling folk were tried in the courts for the practice of sortilege. Divination methods from different cultures are popular today across the same spectrum of people regardless of nationality, or ethnic background. Regionally, the people recognized some common and quite insular ideas regarding signs and omens. In New England, folk magic is employed to protect the dead by observing specific burial rites and regulations that would prevent all manner of bewitchment to the body or soul of the dead.[66] In the Southwest where divination is frequently consulted on holy days,[67] omens and the customs surrounding the deceased meant life or death for the currently living.

-To Read the Future or Divine a Presence:
Mirror (MW, S, SW, SE, NE, CA)
Teacup (G)
Nuts (NE)
Apples (G)
Combs (SE, NE)
Knots, garters and handkerchiefs (G)
Cards (G)
Water Witching Sticks; witch-hazel, persimmon, hickory, willow (S, SE, MW)
Egg-whites, egg-sweating, egg-writing, or egg-breaking (N, S, SW)

-To Predict a Future Lover:
Mirrors, apples, combs, nuts, needles, letters, egg-whites, egg-sweating, garter knots (G), southernwood sprigs (NE, SE, S)
Holly leaf or mistletoe popping (NE)
Clover, daisy, trillium flower counting-out rhymes (G)

Ecstatic and Transfigurative
-To Leave the Body:
Flying ointment (N, NE, SE), witch-butter (S)
Rhymes and incantations (G)

-To Shapeshift:
Flying ointment, "witch's butter", oil or unguent (G)
Witch-bone (S)
Incantations (G)
By wearing a mask or skin in the image of an animal (G)

Erotic

-To Draw Love:

Poppets (G)

Apples (N, NE, SE, CA)

Herbs (G): liverwort (S, SE), Adam and Eve root (S, SE), Trillium (S, NW), Ten-finger plant (S) grape leaf (NE), heartleaf (S), lad's love (S, NE, SE, MW), amaranth seed (S), hemp (NE, SE, S), Clovers (G)

Lodestones fed iron filings to draw a lover (SW, S)

Dove hearts (S, NW, G)

-To Bind Love:

Dollies (G), socks (S, MW, NE),

Knots - *cloth or string knotted for magical purposes likely had several sources when it emerged in America; from English traditional magic in which 9 times knotted cloth was a known love charm, or from the Southwest where Hispanic-Pueblo witches were said to knot cloth to curse enemies (Simmons), or to bind love. Wool, especially red wool, is supposedly the best used to bind charms and tricks* (G)

Talismans involving doves, roses, banners (TA)

Jumping the broom at weddings (AA)

Blood magic of any kind (G); *Ozark folklore reported by Randolph and found in the Hand/Brown Collections recounts that an errant lover could be reclaimed through blood-writing magic on ironwood.*

-To Banish Love:

Foot-track powder (S, SE)

Funereal

-To Lay the Dead to Rest in Honor:

Placing jewelry and flowers *outside* the coffin (NE)

Covering the mirrors of the house (S, SE, NE, MW)

Telling the bees (S, SE, NE, MW)

Opening a window for the dead (G)
Disrupting the grave by robbing it (G)
Dumb-suppers (S, SE, NE)
Spirit Plates (NW, CA)
Pouring out liquor for the dead (G)
Tossing dirt over the closed coffin before burial (G)

Medicinal
-*To Heal:*
Egg (rubbing on body) (SW)
Rubbing stone (S, G)
Bloodroot (S)
Laying hands (G)
Medicine, conjure, root-work, mojo bags (G)

-*For Fertility/Virility:*
Buckeye (S, MW), acorn (G)
Cowrie shell (AA)

The intersectionality of magic between people in the New World is the liminal space where witches like me seek to perfect our tradition of witchcraft. By tracing the ways of our ancestors to the places where their beliefs cross and intersect and parallel one another, this is where we as Americans find our common threads and the unique traditions that could only have been born from such a specific synthesis. This is important for multiracial Americans like myself who seek to draw from the shared traditions of our foremothers, to draw from the places where their beliefs mirrored and connected, right here on the land that brought them together to make us.

Homegrown Hexes: *Churn-Witching, Witch Bullets, and Track Tricks*

Hexing can be an offensive or defensive act, and in witchcraft folklore, there are some pretty standout tools that are long supposed to be used by non-witches and witches alike to do dark deeds. Originating in the folk magic of England, the power of the witch-bottle with its beautiful bellarmine and buried secrets immigrated to the New World. Here, the witch bottles tend to be made of simple glass - filled with nine nails and personal concerns, and are part of both Anglo-American and Afro-American folk magical superstitions of the South. Another hex charm of the Old World is the witch's knot; red cloth that is tied in knots while speaking incantations or prayers in order to lay a trick. Our home-grown hex traditions; witch-bullets and track-tricks are new additions to the great tapestry of witchlore and they've found their way into the folkloric magical practices of New World witches all over the country.

Dairy Demons

A familiar role of the witch in European and American folklore is meddler in the dairy.
- Ronald L. Baker[68]

There's something about witches and butter in the annals of American folk magic. It was serious business that employed serious countermeasures. Appalachian witches of lore were said to be able to milk a rag or even a gooseberry[69] bush to make their butter! One Kentucky story says that a witch left a red rag under a butter churn that caused the butter to stop up.[70] In the Christian folk magical tradition of German Pennsylvania, written charms (including the famed SATOR)[71] charm were given as a talisman for bewitched cattle. Witches were seen as the great bane of dairy, and for whatever reason, witches of folklore were some milk-stealing cattle-haints:

> Witches, or bad women, or women with an evil eye, who have a grudge against a person, by casting the eye on a cow can bewitch the milk so it will not make butter. Cape Breton. (Memoirs of the American Folk-lore Society, 1899, p.22).

Devouring the milk from cows in nightly raids, the turning or stopping-up of the cream, stealing butter on May Day and being a general dairy nuisance - this was witch's work in America, and the only way to stop them was to shoot their image with a silver bullet, or pierce bewitched butter with hot iron or pure silver. While today's witches may not go around haunting the cows and sheep of the farmers, they do still, on occasion, practice hexcraft and our ancestors had ways to deal with witches who tamper with the dairy. Salt was always a recommended recourse to bewitched butter churns, as were hot objects like hot pokers stuck in the cream, thrice-crossed knives, or hot pins, musket-shots fired into the churn, or heated horseshoes; "Put a horseshoe in the fire if your butter won't come and gather. This kills the witches." (FCB, p.443)

Or, you could apply **silver** to the problem; a silver fork, a silver coin like a dime or quarter, or even bless your cattle with silver water to lift any bewitchments off of them that a witch may have used to stop-up the milk or sicken the animal. Silver **bullets** were applied as well. According to accounts from the

Memoirs of American Folk Society, a silver bullet was fired at the image of a witch who was believed to be bewitching the dairy. People of the old days took their dairy very seriously and were willing to defend themselves against the witches who were supposed to be causing the problems.

Witches today can employ the anti-witch properties of these anti-butter-witching charms in their own domestic craft. After all, kitchen witchery is one of the many facets of life deeply touched by our folklore and our cultural heritage and protection of the vital instruments of home and hearth may still hold importance in the lives of witches. But for many of us, protecting our butter isn't high on the priority list, and not a lot of witches are going around spoiling people's butter in the urban environment, but there are still ways to apply to protective attributes of this folk magic in our domestic craft today.

Place a silver coin on the butter shelf, put a pinch of salt in your cannabis butter, stir your milk with a silver fork and watch out for those witches and fairies that fly on May's Eve stealing butter! Witches of the Colonial era were renowned for their fixation with livestock, even going so far as to gather their hair and hex them by firing back their own kind of bullets...

Witch-Bullets and Hairballs

Randolph notes witch balls described as being the size of a marble made of black horsehair, and another one made of black hair and beeswax that was rolled up into a hard pellet. The belief is that a **hairball** *(or witch bullet) could be thrown or shot at a person by a witch. This hairball (or bullet) would be found on the body of anyone killed by this method. (Milnes, 2007, p.168)*[72]

The "witch-bullet" or "witch-ball" (not to be confused with the protective glass "witch-balls" of England), seems to be a syncretic blend of superstitions shared between Indigenous, Africans and Europeans regarding witches with the power to "shoot" or project malicious magics into the body - which took the form of hairballs found in the stomach of livestock and some of the ill. These supposed "bullets" were balls of cattle or horsehair, said to be wound with the hair of an enemy,[73] pins, wax and/or any other manner of malicious object which was then "shot" at the image of an enemy,[74] or, at their livestock, or, at their houses and in their footsteps. Supposedly, people afflicted by the witch's bullet would suffer a great pain before dying. Folklorist Cora L. Daniels reported; *"Witches are supposed to shoot animals with little hairballs, which pass through the hide and lodge, without leaving any hole."*[75] and these little balls would supposedly be found once the victim was examined after death.

Hair is an important part of the body and it was easy to collect from people and animals - it could be used in love charms like knot magic, or, in green magic by splitting a sapling, placing the hair of quarreling lovers in the division and if the wood is to reknit, love would be true.[76] Another for love involves plucking a lover's hair and keeping it on your person (even sewing it into your clothes) to make them love you. According to the *Green Collection*, one should wear a piece of their lover's hair in a locket to make them think of you. An errant lover can be brought home by plugging his hair wrapped around hickory in the doorframe, according to Brown's sources.

Otherwise, hair was a vehicle to cause or return harm to the sender. This witchery appears throughout the folklore of the South, from the Carolinas, Virginia, Alabama, Georgia, Kentucky, Delaware, Tennessee, Iowa, Illinois, Pennsylvania, Maryland to even Michigan and was found in both rural white communities and African American farming communities,[77] interconnecting people by their fear of folks - especially witches.

Actual accounts of witch-bullets being used to harm people and livestock have been recorded throughout the last few hundred years, with reports detailing physical evidence of injury and even naming some of the accused cunning folk, witches, conjurers and sorcerers accused of shooting witch-bullets. This same magic could be used *against* witches in the same manner, just like the silver bullet. Effingham County Illinois folklore references the witch ball as a charm that can be used to counter witchcraft itself.

The hair-ball magical tradition exists within the conjuring traditions as well. Conjure-balls paralleled the witch-bullet hex-lore and was described as a ball of earth gathered from the homestead of the victim, seven or nine bits of hair, a (typically red) knotted rag and the tips of nails and pins. This hex charm is not to be confused with the famed and beneficial *bezoars* of occult history, or with the so-called *'conjure stone'* or snake-stones associated with the protective charms of Southeastern tribes[78] and were likely introduced to outsiders through their own similar notions of "magical stones". Unlike the protective magical "stones" of the Southeasterners, hairball hexes were specifically for the practice of evil or, anti-evil.

A spell was usually worked by means of a conjure ball buried in the victim's path. Bent pins and **human hair** *seem to have been the commonest ingredients, though they were reported to contain snake's tongue, lizard tails, ground puppy claws and so on down the gruesome gamut.* (FCB, 1952, p.101)

These items would be combined together and thrown at a house, above a door, shoved in a chimney or "stobbed" in some wall of the home, or in the path of a victim. Maybe for hate, maybe for love. The conjure-ball was otherwise described as a bundle of red cloth full of similar items which will cause great physical and spiritual ailments. In some Louisiana folklore, the bundle needs to be prepared by a practitioner *for* you; it is dangerous work. In Texas folk medicine, a conjure-ball was to be worn on the person as an apotropaic anti-witch charm. This form of Afro-diasporic magic permeated the lore of hoodoo, voodoo and conjure and found parallels in the Western-European American and Southeast Indigenous projectile magic traditions.[79] Silver bullets, hairball bullets - we are some gun-folk over here, and these tools continue to be used by practitioners today for the same purposes.

Track Tricks

It is said in Knott County, Kentucky, a lover may win his lady's favor by counting her steps up to the ninth, then taking some earth from the track made by her left shoe heel, and carrying it in his pocket for nine days.[80]
- Tom Peete Cross, *Witchcraft in North Carolina*

Most of our track-trick folklore in North America comes from primarily African American folk magical traditions with some European influences (Scottish and English mostly). Witches and conjure folk were believed to gather the tracks of their enemies and *"lay tricks"* on them in order to do harm, or as a defensive measure against harm such as was the case for hot-foot[81] and goofer powders. You may have your tracks laid by anyone with the desire to do so; anyone from Christian folk to sorcerers, to jilted lovers and spurned brides - *anyone* who wanted to do you harm could do so with a little evil work in your footsteps:

*To keep a woman true, take some dirt from her right foot **track** and a wisp of her hair on the back of her neck and stob it in the hole with a hickory stob* (FCB, p.571)

Track-tricks could be the herbs, salt, soil, hair, graveyard soil, nails, thorns, bottles, bags, balls and papers we leave in the tracks of a person, or, they could be the tracks collected themselves which were then tampered with in some way (being boiled, buried, burned or otherwise sweetened or harmed). In many ways, track-tricks of our variety are quite unique; a mixture of African, Indigenous and European mindsets regarding sympathetic magic and contagion. They could seek to get rid of your presence by picking up your tracks and tossing them into running water, or, one could draw (often errant) lovers to themselves by snaring their footprints with specific powdered herbs like liverwort or shame weed:

Shameweed or the sensitive plant will shame a recalcitrant woman; sprinkle the powdered dry root in the woman's path and she will close up like a sensitive plant; mix it with snail dust and snail water and she will leave like a snail going into its shell. (Botkin B.A, 1967, p.663)[82]

Track-tricks and how to lay them can come in a variety of forms with varying instructions; sometimes they take the appearance of "conjure-balls" or similar to "witch bullets", other times they can appear as red-bundles in the middle of the foot-path, or as bottles set into the ground or as cursed objects buried in the earth, placed in the chimney or hidden in the cellar. You could do all kinds of damage just by stealing tracks according to another of Botkin's informants; *"And by a variety of charms involving a person's **tracks,** you may make him stagger or paralyze him, make him follow you or leave."*

While track-tricks aren't always powdered (sometimes they are bundled in bags or hairballs), they most commonly were made up of ground materials to divert evil, some of that powder containing diabolic substances like snakeheads, ground lizard and human body; *"powder made from the dead was strewn in the path of obnoxious individuals to cause them to become ill"* (FCB, p.102). Disturbing the soil left in a person's tracks, or crossing them, or dropping nails into them - a good deal of magic could be done with this magic powder in the American folk magic traditions of African and European Americans. These powders are still popular and easily manufactured today, using recipes both old and new. They serve as a perfect countermeasure and protective charm for those practitioners who do not hex.

The Tides of Witch's Work

Witchcraft practices could be performed whenever, wherever, but the folklore of the early Americas details some fundamental times, places and moon phases that are best suited for witching. A combination of different folk magical beliefs, the tides of the day, month and year as well as the place where witch's work are for the most part pretty specific.

Friday was an evil and unlucky day in the superstitions of early American folklore and quickly became associated with witchcraft, especially in Southern African American folk magical lore - while Wednesday, like Sunday, became associated with goodness and God. In some folklore reports, Friday is an evil day because while witches may *not* work magic that day, they can hear gossip far and wide and report it to the devil.

Liminal spaces like graveyards and crossroads; liminal times like sunrise, sunset and midnight - these all symbolize that deeply seeded fear people have regarding the mysteries of the in-between. Today, New World witches can be inspired in their own crafting by these old traditions, these long-standing traditions that have marked the passage of time within our general culture.

In threes, sevens, and nines
At moons both full and new
At sunset, midnight and twilight
On the Days of Mars and of Venus
Upon Equinoxes Vernal and Autumnal
At Winter and Summer Solstices
During the days that serve witches; Hallows Eve and May Day,
Midsummer and Midwinter
And at those First Fruits and Final Frosts

In sacred and liminal places; graveyards, groves, crossroads, hillsides, mountain caves, cellars and rivers

Seasons Change

The cosmos is a grand clock, one that marks the passage of all of life's cycles. Holy Days, Holidays, Sabbats and Feasts are a special thing to most cultures; a time to celebrate or contemplate; an excuse to bond with loved-ones or the community. When neo-pagans talk about a "Wheel of the Year", they're talking about the change of seasons marked by cosmic phenomena. Those familiar with neo-paganism are likely familiar with *Ostara*, *Imbolc* and *Mabon* - three holy days that may play a prominent role outside of this country, but are not culturally significant where our folklore is concerned. This does not mean they are insignificant to witchcraft today, only that they aren't a part of the developed folklore of our land; we have other days that compensate in some ways, days that do have folk-charms and superstitions in our history (thanks in large part to commercialization) like; Easter, St. Valentine, New Year.

Marking the fluctuations of the yearly cycles connects all people; it is a fundamental clock upon which we rely for our agriculture and livestock. The change of the seasons has long been a herald of the ever-presence of life and death, of the harsh winters and the glorious springs that feed and sustain human cultures. We've built an empire of folk magic and lore to illustrate our faith in the wheel that changes with the passing phases of the moon and stars above. A simple religion.

In our culture today, these pagan hold-fasts correspond to our times of Halloween, Christmas, and Easter. On each holiday we knowingly or unknowingly practice bits of folk magic here and there. The solstices and equinoxes, as well as their surrounding days each have customs, taboos, decor, and menus that inspire our imaginations, and are inspired by our ancestors. We've traded in hillside bonfires at Midsummer for fireworks on July 4th in a way; traded in Yule logs for rotating plastic trees. They are remnants of the pagan festivals of the Old World and their power took root in the New World with gusto, with much thanks to Christianity adopting these once pastoral pagan feasts and giving them a Church-approved purpose as well as the boom of commercialization. The customs we practice at each holiday have social significance for us culturally, and spiritual significance for those practicing folkloric magical traditions.

Hallows Eve, Mays Eve, Midsummer and Midwinter each mark the passage of the seasons and time and each one was ripe with stories, legends, lore and magic, and even witches. It just so happens that the holiday season, each and every season, is decorated in magical superstition, and in witchcraft folklore. On Halloween, witches fly with ghosts and the dead, at Midsummer witches fly over hillsides and on May Day - or rather, on *Walpurgisnacht*, witches were said to fly to an unholy sabbat; and at Midwinter some cultural traditions included charms against fearful spirits who come to unprotected hearths in winter. At each solstice, the common folk of Europe - and later, the Americas, believed that fairies, demons, witches,[83] devils, ghosts, hags and all kinds of terrible and divine magical creatures attended to nefarious deeds and doings, and it was on the layperson to protect themselves during these times of spiritual movement. Love charms were the primary magic of each seasonal holiday, even Christmas and New Year's Eve (when acts of ceromancy and wish-making were a common fortune game among young people at this transitional time.

Modern witches can look towards a combination of customs and superstitions we know and love about each of these holidays to celebrate the passage of the year and to take advantage of the power these liminal times had in the eyes of some of our ancestors. These can be connected with our secular and cultural practices and help promote new traditions in our modern families (especially for those who wish to free themselves from the material aspect of holidays.

Some ideas for bringing folk-magic back into your seasonal celebrations:

Midsummer; during the Eve of St. John, go bathe in a river or lake to purify yourself for this sacred day which witches fly. Go into the woods to gather fern seeds; dance around the fern with the fairies and the Black Man of the Crossroads. Gather St. John's Wort to hang in the home, and gather nine different kinds of flowers to place under your pillow before you sleep. Weave and toss flower wreaths with friends and strew herbs of fertility and sun.

All Hallows Eve; set a Silent Supper for your Dead; this was known as a 'dumb supper', which, in American folklore, has more of an association with love projects. Some witches have adapted this method from a project in which young girls would set a dinner at night backwards and leave empty chairs to be filled by the portent of their future husband, into a ritual to honor the beloved dead by setting a place for the dead and eating in silence to honor them. And other times, you set no space for the dead; you eat in silence, blow out the candles and the face of your intended will appear on the plate. The dumb supper need not always be totally silent, as per one charm; silently set a table at 11 p.m. with bread and butter and silver knives and forks (again, silver's importance in magical work) and when the clock strikes midnight, say, "Whoever my true love may be, come and eat this supper with me."

Frank C. Brown and Wayland Hand's collection of Dumb Supper lore of North Carolina and nearby States involve the "sweating" of an egg in a fire in order to summon a lover to come and "turn" the egg in the fire before your very eyes, other instructions say that guests are to eat and retire without speaking and they will have premonitions of their intended lovers. Or, at midnight, go to some sacred place like a graveyard, the woods, a riverside or cave, to dance and play love games with apple seeds and fire popping nuts and needles in a dish of water. Steal cabbages from fields at midnight and make general mischief to rile the spirits of the living and dead. Before bedtime, walk backwards outside, pick up a bit of grass and soil, wrap it in paper and place it under your pillow to dream of the future.[84]

Additional Hallows Charms (which can also be practiced at Midsummer, May Day and New Year's):

Love Twine Charm

"Throw a ball of yarn into an unoccupied house, and holding the end of the yarn, wind, saying, "I wind and who holds?" The one who is to be your future wife or husband will be seen in the house."[85]

Love Apple Charm

Count the apple seeds you collect on Halloween from your bobbing apple with this old folk-charm from the Frank C. Brown Collection;

"One, I Love; two, I love; three, I love, I say,
Four, I love with all my heart; five, I cast away.
Six, he loves; seven, she loves,
Eight, they both love.
Nine, he comes; ten, he tarries,
Eleven, he courts; twelve, he marries.
Thirteen, honor, fourteen, riches;
All the rest are little witches!"[86]

Mirror Charm

"On the last night of October, take a mirror and a clock in a room that has not been used for some time, and at a quarter to twelve take a lighted candle and an apple, and finish eating the apple just as the clock strikes twelve and then look in the mirror and you will see your future husband."[87]

Midwinter; *decorate the home in evergreens (all but those of yew or ivy) to welcome the spirits of the green. Burn a fire throughout the solstice to symbolize the return of the sun, and, to keep away malevolent spirits on the long night. Perform holly leaf divinations by counting their points for "love-me-nots" and hang mistletoe from the eaves and doorways. Bring holly indoors for good tidings and count your luck by the berries that fall before New Year's. Pop hollies or mistletoe leaves before the fireplace, naming each leaf for your suitors. Christmas as a secular Western tradition is still popular, and one good way to decenter the materialistic/commercial aspect of this season is to bring some folk traditions back into the focus which include gathering for games and feasting, singing, keeping all-night fires in the hearth and protecting the home.*

May's Eve/May Day; *in the morning on the eve of May, gather dew from beautiful flowers - hawthorn, rose, periwinkle, violet, or daisy is best. On May Day morning, wash yourself in this dew; the concept of getting wet on the first day of May and particularly of collecting the dew of flowers on may's eve is a European branch and has influenced our May Day folklore in the States. Additionally, common folklore of European origin regards the dew of May Morning as particularly effective in bestowing beauty upon the lad or lady who bathes in the dew. Look for wells and divine by them with mirrors' holding the mirror up as you look over your shoulder and into the well. Dance around fires and feed butter and bread to the fairies (if you've got them) to keep them appeased.*

Additionally, **New Year** and **St. Valentine's Day** have folk-charms associated with their celebration in our country, some of which we know very well. Come St. Valentine's day, our world is covered in scarlet and blush, roses and carnations, milk chocolate and sexual innuendo. We utilize the language of followers in conveying our love, friendship or desire to those around us, we play love-games and pick the petals off daisies to see if we will or will not be loved. New Year has some particularly fun folk charms, taboos and customs, like those recorded by Emrich in *The Hodgepodge Book: An Almanac of American Folklore* (1972); never throwing anything out on New Year's day, sleeping with a horseshoe under your pillow and making a wish, leaving a loaf of bread, coins and salt on the table to usher in wealth and prosperity come the New Year - even being sure to eat symbolic foods for good luck in the year to come. The Wheel of the Year for a New World witch is bound to be a unique and personal thing, reflecting their own ideas of family and culture, their own ideas of what marks the passage of time or draws together loved ones. It may be high time to re-evaluate just what the Wheel means today, to us.

Chapter 6

Hags Riding with Familiars

The Witch's Skin and The Witch's Ride

The Modern American witch, though perhaps not quite as malignant as her predecessors, is fully equipped with a wide range of uncanny powers. Like the witches of all time, she is a shapeshifter of astonishing versatility.[88]

- Tom Peete Cross, *Witchcraft in North Carolina*

Witches are creatures of spirit more than anything else and this is true in most cultures. A witch is a thing of the spirit-world; a person in league with the unseen and invisible forces we fear in the world. The transformative, transfigurative nature of the witch permeated most cultures, and when the Old World met the New, this commonality was a deeply shared fear. African, European and Indigenous witchlore share all the common aspects of power and maliciousness, not least among them, the shared faith in a witch's ability to change shape and to leave their bodies by spirit. Both methods of spiritual transport captured the imaginations and fears of our early American ancestors. The skin-walking witch could transform themselves or leave their own skin behind while they traveled in some unholy form, or, they could send their spirit out as their bodies lay dead to the world to do their deeds and serve their masters:

Supernatural animals were not always familiars, for witches were assumed to have the power of transfiguration or the ability to change into bestial form. This metamorphosis enables witches to roam about undetected by humans and to do foul deeds without fear of discovery. (Booth, 1975, p.36)[89]

The idea that the moths that were fluttering up the chimney at night were actually the spirits of their sleeping wives or the thought of finding a witch's skin after they slipped from their bodies was unbearable to many rural folks. Witches were thought, in the early colonies among both Europeans settlers and African slaves, to be responsible for enchanting cattle at night, feeding from dairy cows and sheep to steal all of the milk, and riding (known as Hagriding) people quite literally, through the night - and this they could achieve through transfiguration. The witch's mount of choice was most often animal more so than a broomstick - goats, horses, birds, and usually with no more than the uttering of an incantation or formula. Horses were a clear favorite of American witches; they were reported to transform people into horses at night and ride them across the land on errands, or worse, they'd leave their victims as humans and make them ride about:

> If real horses were unavailable for Hagriding, colonials believed that witches would substitute human beings for natural steeds. Sometimes the victims were physically transformed into horses but in most cases, the unfortunate settlers were left in human form while being known as a "nightmare". (Booth, Sally, p.43)

In Afro-American lore, she is a Hag-riding skin-slipper, and to Europeans, she could choose to change her form or leave her body behind entirely. Both points-of-view held witchcraft traditions well known for their ability to slip-the-skin and traverse the space between worlds through spirit, on their breath, in the night. Hags, which are a class of spirit-witch, are regularly equated or, at the very least associated with human witches in most cultures, and this didn't change in the Americas.

Many, if not most Indigenous American tribes had their own figures that paralleled or resembled witches, and sometimes they were very dangerous, shape-shifting, cannibalistic night-riders - however, the exact origin of the folklore we've recorded among Southeast tribes have questionable roots. According to Alan Kilpatrick and other ethnographers, tribes like the Cherokee shared in similar beliefs as Europeans and African Americans regarding spirits, but it may very well have been contact with Europeans that disseminated this notion into this tribe:

> *To the Cherokee mind, this capacity for the magical transformation of physical form (whether human or animal) appears to be one of the most telling characteristics of the witch. The woods of northeastern Oklahoma are alive with stories of witches soaring through the sky as illuminating balls of fire, a trait thought by some ethnographers to have been introduced from European folklore (Parsons 1939, 1065-68) but which is found among widely dispersed Native American groups living in the southwest (Simmons 1980, 57-58) and in the northeast (Shimony 1989, 150).*(Kilpatrick, 1997, p.8)[90]

The basket-Ogresses and Snail-Women of Coastal Salish story-telling were hags; the Gullah feared boo-hags who rode victims at night and stole their breath like vampires; the very Germanic word *hag* is in reference to witches. Often in our Southern folklore, she/he rides men in their sleep in the form of a spirit, familiar, shadow, haunt or devil, bridle[91] and all.

By Bridle,[92] Broom and Butter-Dasher,[93] the witches and hags could fly from their bodies or their homes in many ways. A popular aspect of witch-flight lore is the use of a substance which is rubbed on the body by a witch; a concoction such as an ointment or grease or, "witch-butter",[94] that will help the witch "slip" their skins.

> *Through thick, through thin; 'way over in the hagerleen,*[95]

Though Flying Ointments as we know them are a distinctly

Old World charm, they became part of the witchlore of many Americans, and just as in Europe, the ointment of an American witch was made of some diabolic substances; snakes, baby-fat, corpse materials, noxious herbs, etc. With a simple incantation, the witch would fly from their bodies or from their homes out into the night. She would cry as she leapt from her skin, *"I, into the keyhole."* or, *"Into the keyhole I go!"* or, *"Through the keyhole I go!"* and away she would fly. And upon her return to her skin she would cry, *"Skin don't you know me? Skin don't you know me, jump out and jump in!"*[96]

We have always left our bodies; on a single breath, by changed flesh, by total transformation or spirited-dream in order to wander in the night for our work. By narcotic smokes and mind-altering ointments; by snake-butters and flying ointments we leave our forms behind and ride the night and those misfortunate enough to lay beneath us. It is the ecstasy that we seek; that's the allure of the woodland sabbat or the hallows eve silent supper; of the night-ride and the spirit flight - we are the thing that crosses those worlds, something all witches share, all over the country and beyond.

Today's witches keep the traditions of spirit flight alive through the revival of "flying ointments" and the implementation of new trance and meditative techniques. The idea of a witch as a literal shapeshifter may have all but disappeared in current superstition, but the belief in those who can move their spirits between worlds is still a heavily emphasized aspect of folkloric religious traditions in the Americas.

Faithful Factotum

The most important creatures in American witchlore were familiars, demon servants that took the form of living animals in order to surreptitiously serve the enchanters. Familiars were indispensable in the practice of magic. Not only did the creatures assist witches in casting spells, but by disguising themselves as normal beats of wilderness, the spirits could move undetected through the countryside, spying upon innocent citizens and performing evil assignments. (Booth, 1975, p.32)

A familiar or ally spirit, regardless of physical or incorporeal form, is an intrinsic aspect of witchcraft, especially in the lore of the New World, in which witches were supposed to have done most of their deeds through the work of vermin familiars and invisible allies (some call devils).

The witch was allied to rats and toads, frogs and crows, all manner of insect and rodent, even to deer and horses (nightmare). The witch could slip her skin and leave the home as a moth, or a beetle, she could send a cat out with her own eyes in its skull and fly from house to house as a ball of fire in the night.[97] Whatever the beast, a witch's spirit often required a herald, a guide or an ally to aid it in their work. In much of witchlore, one's pact with the Devil would inevitably lead to the gifting of a familiar spirit as well as the means by which a witch could transform himself into the likeness of his faithful factotum.

In all lore I've researched; from the heart of West Africa to the tip of Northern Europe and over here throughout every single region from the tip of Alaska to the tip of Argentina, the witch is always and intrinsically connected to a familiar spirit. This is most prevalently a servant or guide or both, in the form of an animal, object or natural phenomenon. In the synthesis of folklore that created the motif of the witch in the New World, the witch's companion was most often a creature of devilish and horrific form, a specter, an imp, or, an animal of dark tidings like a black cat, crow, fly, rabbit, beetle, snake, etc.

Incubi and succubi were not at all unheard of in the witchcraft fears of places like Pennsylvania and Southeastern Virginia - these types of spirits would be known to assume the form of a spouse and take their place in bed while the witch-spouse attended a "diabolical errand".[98] The spirits that work in league with witches may take the shape of beasts or goblins, trolls or shadows, ghosts or plant-spirits; there really is no limit to the relationships a witch may forge with forces of this world and of the other side.

Land, Water and Sky
Familiars and Their Haunts

Land

When we think of witches, we think of horned demons, little imps, and particular animals, and each of the ones we associate has a good reason for being so. Rabbits took the place of hares in the New World as the witch's lagomorph of choice; witch rabbits and graveyard rabbits who bring ill-luck in every regard but their hind feet and are referenced throughout the collections of American witchcraft folklore as the servants of spirits, heralds of ill omens and forms taken by evildoers in the night. Witches, fairies, and ghosts were all supposed to take rabbit or hare's form in both Old and New World folklore, and in the Americas, they could not be killed by a simple means,[99] but by a silver bullet only; and even then, the act of killing a witch rabbit was as dangerous in the New World as it had been in England and Scotland.[100]

I shall go intill a hare, With sorrow and sych and meikle care...[101]

Cats, as always, are accused of doing the witches' bidding, as are mice, white horses and all manner of cattle and goat. Cats are a well-known medium of the witch to transform into or familiar with but they are not at all the most well-known - *lycanthropy* of any kind is a witch's art, one reported from all over the country[102] and existed among tribes of the Southwest and Northeast[103] even before interaction with settlers. The witch would feed their familiars offerings of blood or food in exchange for service as it was believed that familiars would not or could not do their workings without nourishment.[104] Those animals who are pests to the crops and the kitchen were thought to be serving dissatisfied witches seeking revenge. The familiars of New World witches were not always large predators like wolves, coyotes, and black dogs, but also smaller ones; cats, rats, mice, flies, gnats and foxes[105] (foxes being a beloved familiar of Southwestern witches according to Sullivan). The animals that could do the most spying and infiltration, that most represented the cunning ways of life; these were the familiars connected to witchcraft.

Spirits of the crossroads; like the Witchking, the Witchqueen, Hags and hounds, the banjo devils and familiar spirits are spirits of the land; the shadows between the trees, the subterranean nursery from which the seeds of life emerge; this is where the liminal gods reside. The infernal spirits and otherworldly creatures that are known for their night flying cavorting with witches and their alliances with our craft dwell in the in-between places that most people fear to go. Root familiars dwell here; they, the heart and soul of the whole herb is where most of the power resides and we harvest these not just for their practical applications but for their long-standing comradery with practitioners of medicinal and magical arts alike.

The spirits of the crossroads are not the foes of the practitioner; they are the teachers of cunning and witching folk, and they are part of the land and its mysteries - just as witches are part of the land and its mysteries. In my tradition, the crossroads is the place for all of the spirits to cross paths, and it serves a ritualistic meaning in my work; symbolizing the pathways between worlds, between people, between spirits.

Snake witches appear a bit in folklore; those who take the forms of snakes or send them out to do their bidding. The snake is not just an Old World familiar; it can be found in familiarity with witches in Japanese and African folklore as well. In the

Southwest, witches' familiars could be coyotes, beetles, moths or lizards, or snakes, and in the Pacific Northwest, the cannibal witches are sometimes associated with snakes and snails. Even using snakes by proxy or by image in contagion or sympathetic magic charms or rituals could have the effect of poisoning, harming according to conjurelore.

Among the earthly creatures of the night associated with witches and witchcraft itself were the werewolves. The wolf witches of Ginzburg's *Night Battles* that haunted the Old World farmlands and livestock were found in the New World as well. The lycanthropy of the witch is often associated with the use of herbal agents - an ointment perhaps; one of monkshood and mallow, thornapples and goose fats,[106] one that will make you appear as in a stupor but send your spirit forth in flight. The folktales of witches who could turn into wolves or turn others into wolves was found even in the Midwest[107] among French Americans, and those werewolves who haunted the night were in league with witches - or were witches themselves.

Water

Toads, who have long associations with the cunning folk in some parts of England, have a fair share of superstition around them in the states as well as being witch's companions. This mythology extends to frogs, kinds of lizards and other moist and slithering creatures that may well in water.

Mother of Oceans; The folklore of the water has a special deity, a holdover from our seafaring maritime days; the mermaid. The seafaring life was one of great importance to our folklore and our history - those who came here sailed treacherous seas full of peril and strangeness. Its depths were the source of endless song and rhyme, superstition and story. We're descended from that history of the sea, of the wonders of the untamable deep. Maritime folklore and superstition shape the unique pocket-cultures of our coasts, the same in Canada and Mexico and the

Caribbean. The sea and all its mystery is home to our oldest fears and wonders about the world, and the most widespread mystery was that of the Lady of the Ocean.

Mami Wata, La Sirene, Yemanja, and the Mermaid; there are a good deal of water-mother spirits and they permeate every aspect of coastal folklore across our shores and each culture has their own version of this court of water spirits. In the Americas, she is symbolic of beauty, travel, and death[108] and is part of our naval symbolism and traditional American artwork. This cryptid has the distinguished honor of being our choice symbol of oceanic mythology, representing wealth, beauty, mystery, death and exploration.

West and Central African cultures had a wide array of ancient water deities - usually females, who were both kind and cruel, cunning and vain. Europeans shared this view of the oceanic femme fatal in their mermaid folklore. In the New World, La Sirene, the half-fish/half-woman/man is a commonly observed figure of artistic (and spiritual) importance seen in beach town souvenir shops and maritime lore in every beach coast from the Atlantic to the Gulf to the Pacific. The merwoman is also a popular sea spirit in the Maritimes[109] and in New England, something I've enjoyed learning about throughout Connecticut and Rhode Island - she's a folk feature in Mystic Connecticut, a symbol of the seafaring life in Salem Massachusetts. In the Gulf States, she is Mami Wata, Yemanja and La Sirene among those associated with Voodoo and African/Latino diasporic spiritual traditions.

These days, her symbolism in witchcraft as a spirit of water and entity of magic has ingrained itself into the folkloric traditions of some witches and it's easy to see why, given her universal nature among all kinds of cultures - not to mention her symbolism to sea-loving Americans. For witches of coastal towns, the spirits of the sea, especially those who resemble the mer-folk make for accessible friends and familiar spirits.

Sky

The symbolism of the Owl as a herald of death is found among a great deal of Indigenous tribes; from the Pueblo lore of the Southwest[110] to the Hesquiaht of the Pacific Northwest, the owl's symbolism as a portent of death and witchcraft[111] is shared with the Yoruba, Cherokee and with most European folk beliefs. The owl is the witch of bird-kind and a familiar to the Hags of the world; really most manner of nocturnal bird holds association with witches who themselves were said to do their work most commonly by night. Whether the Witchqueen is An Cailleach, Lilith, Owl-Woman or even Hekate, the owl (especially the screech owl) is a famed witch and a witch's familiar, capable of foretelling or bringing death. Crows, ravens and all blackbirds are likewise associated with witching in general lore as they were "harbingers of death".[112]

Don't you hear the jay bird's call?
Don't you hear them dead sticks fall?
He's a thrown down firewood for we all;
All on a Friday morning.
- *Frank C. Brown Collection*[113]

Not every familiar out there in the world of witching is *your* familiar. Some belong to the Witchking himself. Just as rabbits and mice and horses were said to serve the Hags of night, so is the Devil served by spirits too, and in the American South and Southeast, a curious bluebird is His familiar and the jay serves both our Witchking and us as a liminal force, an intermediary. The devil-lore of this bird is found in Maryland, Illinois, Texas, Michigan and even Colorado thanks to the Great Migration. This marvelously loud and beautiful bird was said by some in the Ozarks and Carolinas to carry twigs, sand and Sulphur to the Devil every Friday to stoke the fires of hell, or, he would spy on sinners all week and tell the Devil on Friday, that he may know of man's sinning.[114] Otherwise, one could even summon the blue jay by leaving corn kernels around a hollowed tree stump and petitioning the Devil through him for some weeks until the master himself appears to train you.

Southerners say that the blue jay was yoked to a plow by a sparrow. The mark left by the yoke can still be seen on the blue jay's breast.
- Laura C. Martin, *The Folklore of Birds*[115]

The jay-bird is a trickster spirit, a psychopomp who moves between worlds, a servant of that man-at-the-crossroads who so loves his witches. It is divine tattletale and historical reporter whose service to witches include informing the Devil of our petitions and apprising him to the sinful goings-on of the world in which the witch works their deeds. How the blue jay became this folk hero of the Devil's work in the first place is a bit of a mystery, but the blue jay, like the blue flame, seems to have represented the Devil's hold in this world especially within African American spiritual superstitions of the South and Southeast.

Fridays were the blue jay and the Devil's day in early American folklore of the South, and especially of his witches and familiars, and so it was widely believed that one would not usually see a blue jay on Fridays for that was when he flew to hell with his offerings. The blue jays' symbolic relationship with the Devil is not as his servant as much as he's a messenger, a trickster, a tattletale, but it was believed that you should be careful of who you offend on Fridays, because the blue jay just may tell the Devil on you.

Sacred Spirits of the skies include the spirits of the dead; those beings that fly by night and haunt the living. The spirits who ride with witches, who sometimes *are* witches themselves, fill the sky with their howls and their wonder. Ghosts, spirits, fellow witches even could be familiar with witches. Whatever fills the wind with magic in the night, upon air and darkness, was friend to the witch.

Chapter 7

A Green Heart

Deep Green Roots

Animism, the earliest form of spiritual belief, operated on the principle that each and every object in nature possessed both a tangible and an ethereal dimension and that the one could not be separated from the other, whether the primitive eye was viewing a mammoth, a mountain or a tree.
- Michael Jordan, *The Green Mantle*

Herbalism plays an intrinsic role in our society's perception of nature and health and has been a leading facet of magical practice since the dawn of time. Knowledge of medicinal and poisonous plants and their use is part of the collective consciousness of every culture and is a form of science that transcends "race, religion, gender, and culture. The witches of the New World consort with spirits and secret knowledge of the magical and spiritual natures of plants and places and things. This assumption that the world is inhabited by unseen spirits is the longest-held belief in history and its persistence even into the modern era says a lot about the spiritually naturalistic way that we continue to see the world. Folk magic covers every foundation of everyday life and how to treat the ailments within it, or the fear of what comes after. In the folk magical mind, all plants have some medicinal or magical application. In Western occult traditions, plants are often ascribed tremendous powers in combination and are given all manner of correspondence. In the low magic of the common folk, the natural world is viewed intuitively and traditionally, blending personal experience with handed-down medicinal knowledge.

It was once customary in American agrarian practices of some Western European settlers and their descendants to plant according to the phases of the moon, but the witch or the cunning person would not need the boundaries of fields and hedgerows for their work - they were the ones who were said to be found wandering the hillside collecting herbs. Witches in particular were feared because they knew the spirits of herbs and tended to haunt wild places where strange ferns, roots and fungi grow. They knew the poisons that enchant and ensnare foolish men and the ones that render them dead. Some plants were long regarded as witches in spirit and function themselves, like mandrake and thorn apple; others were conjurors such as Low and High John, and others were said to be where the Devil gathered; ferns, willows, elders and fairy-rings.

Nature; unbridled and without a master is the only force we can prove without a doubt through observation carries an absolute power over our lives and our choices. It is indiscriminate, genderless, all-encompassing and without bias. As the hurricane rips apart homes so does it fling new life on to remote islands, giving way to new ecosystems and forms of life. And just as our elders are taken from us after withering away, so does nature give us the very ability to make children, full of potential. And really, that's what the beauty in animism and land veneration is, it is the art of acknowledging the potential within the smallest seed or the greatest storm to make something unpredictable and new, in all its terror and wonder.

Our animistic ancestors saw spirits within the land; within stones and trees, within mountains and grottos and groves. They personified the divine through nature, or rather, personified nature as divine. Natural functions and phenomenon over time took on multiple related aspects, names, stories and entire sagas. The mysteries of thunder, tides and seasons mystified our ancestors and gave way to the first religions of man. These days, people know a great deal more about nature, evolution and the natural sciences of physics and chemistry and yet are no less mystified by the incredible force of creation and destruction we call Nature.

When it comes to green spirituality, and more specifically, the metaphysical side of it where concepts like *magic* become a focus, I believe we should place an emphasis on our ancestors, in learning from their green arts to better our own. Our Latin American, European, African, Asian and Indigenous ancestors shared some deep commonalities on a folk magical level, especially when it comes to the ways of herbs, trees and fungi and this wasn't lost even as monotheism took hold. Within the folk magical mind, the idea of an inherent spirit to things; that trees and roots and herbs and even minerals can attain some otherworldly quality, or are in fact spirited things by nature. When we work with the spirits of plants and implement their medicine and magical properties as our ancestors have long done, we are tapping into this universal expression of naturalism within human cultures; this veneration and understanding for the land and what it produces.

The Green Paths Meet

Many witches, under torture, confessed to using herbs roots, leaves and powders to harm man and beast; and although that proves

nothing as to their guilt, it does suggest that they were at home in folk medicine.[116]
- Norman Cohn, *Europe's Inner Demons: An Enquiry Inspired by the Great Witch Hunt*

Most authors who've written detailed accounts of American witchcraft history tend to agree that the perceptions we have as a society of witches and the folklore we enjoy today is a byproduct of European religious superstition and folk customs, Indigenous American medicine and West African spiritualities. From the very beginning, enslaved Africans and Indigenous Americans exchanged agrarian knowledge which lent itself to the history of agricultural production of the Americas. Europeans had a tertiary understanding of the New World plants familiar in likeness to those found back in their homelands, and marveled at the incredible abundance of this side of the world. But this strange world was also full of strange new and poisonous herbs that were responsible for all manner of ailment and malady for the early colonizers. As each culture interacted with one another, under conditions both foul and fair, the exchange of medical knowledge was immediate.

Traditional medicine permeates most cultures. Because medicine is a pursuit tied to both science and spirit, we see cross-cultural parallels frequently between the medicinal and magical uses of herbs in everyday life. People understand health; we understand the need for medicine and our survival, and the New World with all its new people and new diseases, became a hot-bed of shared medicinal lore. This is the place where we start to see full syncretism in the traditional medicine of the people, giving way to American herbal medicine which is a blend of every kind of medicine imaginable. Herbs, such as trillium find use in love charms in both Southern hoodoo and in traditional Coastal Salish medicine[117] - neither having impacted the other. Roses serve the same protective and cleansing qualities in the Northwestern traditional remedies[118] as they seem to in the English pharmacopoeia. Plants with verifiable medicinal qualities like willow, poppy and yew are used similarly by the cultures which are familiar with these plants, and used in similar ways to treat similar medical issues. The exchange of herbal medicinal information is a complicated subject all its own.

Native American ethnobotany has been invaluable to the survival of people during and after the Colonial era, and the information was easily recognized by cultures who shared similar traditions of medicine. Traditional medicine is an integral aspect of Indigenous life in the Americas, as well as Indigenous religions. Mesoamericans had an astounding pharmacopoeia[119] that included all manner of plant, mineral and animal materials used in the treatment of common ailments; this wasn't uncommon among different tribal groups of the Americas - traditional medicine was far more advanced here than modern science likes to credit, and it is, in part, *because* of Indigenous American medicine that settlers and slaves were able to survive in the New World.

As American expansion and immigration grew, Eastern traditions of herbalism became a strong influence on all aspects of herbal medicine in the States. Information is the most valuable resource for cultural survival, and the parallels we see between people and their ethnobotanical information illustrates just how much our ancestors had in common; for example; there are incredibly similar parallels between Chinese traditional herbalism and traditional medicine of the California Chumash[120] including nearly identical uses for similar or related herbs and their administration medicinally. Likewise, there are striking similarities between the African and Native American plant medicines; namely the animistic and spiritual value assigned to plants and those who gather them.

West African and Native American traditions of medicine tended towards a deeply spiritual mind-set, and both tended to hold deep consideration for the divine attributes[121] that inhabit the plant world, those attributes giving the plant its power and spirit. Diasporic Afro-American spiritual systems place a huge emphasis on the importance of plant spirits and herbal medicine in treating all maladies be they spiritual or physical- something inherited from the animistic religions of their ancestors who had originated on the Ivory and Gold Coasts, Senegal and Gambia, Congo and Angola, Nigeria and Cameroon.[122] These people came from different parts of the African continent and had very different religions operating within their cultures, but something they all shared was a sense of the spiritual value of plants and the natural world and this was preserved in a fashion in the agrarian and medicinal information that was passed on through black American families and the folk magic of the American South.[123]

The knowledge of agrarian practices by West Africans brought to the New World is depressingly underrated; black contributions to American society in general tend to be overlooked outside of Black History Month and medicinal knowledge as well as herbal contributions by Afro Americans is one of the lesser known aspects of our history. We owe the introduction and production of peanuts and okra in the Americas to Africa as well as sustainable farming techniques which increased productivity on Southern farms and we know that West African slaves are primarily responsible for United States' economic prosperity through their labor in the cotton, corn and tobacco industries throughout the Americas. It wasn't a choice. We *know* this deep history but we don't celebrate the contribution of black American agriculture in as positive a way as we should. We tend to gloss over the intellectual and economic contributions of black Americans because we're viewing it through a lens of ignorance regarding black history; we don't often take the time to acknowledge that this stability we all currently enjoy was largely built by African Americans upholding the very industries that gave the United States our economic foothold in history.

By the Colonial era, Europe had long sought to turn away from the magical medicine of plants to the hard science, and often saw the ritualistic practices by Natives regarding plant life as indicative of sorcery and poisoning. Despite this, the folkloric heart of herbalism remained strong among European settlers and found parallels with local and African herbalism. When Europeans first encountered the wonders of the New World, they also encountered a great deal of plants whose properties, portions and poisonous natures were a complete unknown to colonizers. What Europeans encountered in the New World was an entirely foreign pharmacopoeia, the mysteries of which were known only to the Indigenous inhabitants.

While much of the knowledge that Indigenous people taught the early settlers had been considered a *savage,* even *evil* art, one that engendered terror in settlers, a great deal of what they taught the colonizers became invaluable for European survival in the New World. This was further complemented by the exchange of agrarian information and traditional medicine between African slaves in the Caribbean and the surrounding Indigenous tribes - and later, between slaves on the mainland and local tribes with whom there is an extensive history of intermarrying. Both groups were under siege and left to survive this harsh new reality, and one of the ways the mutual survival of African and Indigenous folk medicinal knowledge could be ensured was to disseminate this information through family, church and community and share it between peoples during commerce and trade. Coupled with the folk medical knowledge of the Europeans, the first vestiges of American herbal folk medicine grew and the witchlore of plants along with it.

Stewardship

We are people of the land descended from people of the land. Many atrocities soaked this soil, and many people sacrificed their soil, and today we all benefit from that dark history of oppression. We owe it to our ancestors to care for this land and value the life that walks upon it. We can honor the sacrifices of our ancestors by honoring the health, stability and conservation of this land. By fighting for fair land rights, by supporting sacred land rights of Indigenous Americans, by supporting the efforts of Indigenous peoples to protect water and land from overconsumption and pollution - and this starts with recognizing the sovereignty of our Indigenous people. Supporting cleanup efforts, donating to conservation efforts made by local tribes and remembering to walk humbly on the land will help us change our culture for the better.

We can steward this land by supporting local urban gardeners who promote permaculture in their communities in an effort to combat all manner of social ailment from food deserts to obesity, from food addiction to scarcity. We can participate in restorative efforts to local habitats threatened by pollution, and we can support the stabilization of protected land rights for endangered species; not just for animals but for plants and fungi as well. We can honor our history by acknowledging the atrocities that brought us here and working tirelessly to do better for the generation we raise.

The effort we put into honest understanding of the past and progressive pursuit of an equitable future for us all will shape the landscape, and the bones that rest within it. Our ancestors, this land and our individual liberty upon it is a cultural imperative for us, it is part of our way of life. When we own up to our past mistakes and learn from them, we can move forward and sew something in this land that is new and good and fair. An acknowledgment of the Spirit is at the heart of magic; this inherent animism permeates our art and our faith, and working towards a balanced service to the ancestors and the land is part of our cultural identity.

When we work with plants as medicine, we must do so with respect to the future use and preservation of the plant; when we work with plants as spirits, we must do so with respect to their personalities, natures or souls; when we work with plants as magic, we must do so with respect to the consequence of their potential power. Modern witches tend to work with all three facets of plant spirit medicine and depending on who you are and what you believe, this will influence the taboos, customs and practices you follow in the planting, finding, gathering and uses of plants.

The Green Spirits

As entities of the spirit world, plants have innate powers to influence human destiny and fortune. This influence can be negative or positive, depending upon the actions and attitudes of the people who encounter them. Thus, plants can bring good fortune and success in hunting, fishing, root digging, berry picking, basketry, or canoe making. Plants can also protect people against evil forces, illness, or even death. On the other hand, if people neglect to show appropriate respect and appreciation in their actions, and if they disregard certain taboos or constraints, plants can cause serious harm to them. The same is true of animals, rivers and mountains. (Turner, 2014, p.315)

The spirits of plants are the allies of the shaman, healer and witch alike; aiding in visionary traditions and magic work. In the folkloric traditions of the New World plants have a prominent role in the facilitation of magic, in rituals, in medicine, and in every other aspect of life. While many people today recognize the term "green witch" as a modern phrase describing witches whose work solely revolves around plant-spirit animism and occult herbalism, a green witch isn't a *new* figure. What were once called cunning folk, grannies, healers, charmers and even conjurors and hoodoo-folk, were in fact practicing the green arts in accompaniment or as a manifestation of their crafts.

In the magical garden grows creeping vines and some very

bitter roots. It could be a place of tobacco fields or the low toadstools beneath the birch. A witch's garden may be a place of flowering cacti and dust covered sagebrush along the hillsides, or it could be a wet, dark undergrowth wood along the cold northern seas. The gardens of our magic are reflected in the land upon which we live, the place where we live. The folk magician who knew the plants of their region for magic or medicine were a thing of legend. In the Southwest, the *curanderos* and *yerberas* were famed for their knowledge of where and how to use plants to heal and to bless, treat el *mal de ojo* and *susto*.[124] In the Northeast and the South, folkloric records detail accounts of folk healers both of good and ill repute who did many wonders by means of herbal magic and plant spirit wisdom.

There can be no *Santeria* without herbs, there can be no *brujeria* without herbs, there can be no *medicine* without herbs - there can be no access to the spiritual powers of plants without the say-so of the spirit world or the divine; there can be no great healing work without the spiritual participation of the natural world around us, particularly those of plant life and fungi. It is as natural in the witchlore of Western and Northern Europe as it is among the Coastal Salish to leave offerings and tokens of appreciation for specific herbs when harvesting - recognition of the herb spirit's power and the respect between the plant-worker and the plant itself.

The spirit of the plant - the soul within the root, the life within the being, is the magic we are working with as witches, and in the New World, witches were well versed in the most vicious of plants; those that could do the most harm and the most good.

Usually associations of *poisoning* and witches in the New World were the result of hysteria and misunderstandings of African and Indigenous folk religious practices in the New World by the colonizers, but there is a long-standing history around the world associating people who practice magic (good or bad) with the power of plants - in fact, magical folk are always associated with the spirits and the spirits of plants. That is what witchcraft is; the folk art of the spiritual and natural worlds and that which lies between them.

The New World Garden

There were a tremendous number of taboos associated with herbs, their gathering, their growing and their storing. Some herbs were well-known for being medicinally useful, while others were only ascribed spiritually useful qualities. Some of the best medicines are poisons, some of the most foul-smelling plants offer the sweetest remedies. The herbs of love tended to be sweet and beautiful, the herbs of hate were spiny and thorned, the herbs of witching; these were vast. Witch-hazel, persimmon, blackthorn, hickory, alder and, willow; witching trees were many, and beyond the trees, there were many herbs who were far more well known for their magical and symbolic qualities (clovers, violets) than their medicinal value.

Herbal folklore in the Americas has some patron plants and spirits of choice and they represent the full array of **indigenous**, **introduced** and **invasive** medicinal-magical herbs. Those three aspects of the plant world parallel the history of the times in many ways, and though (like history) some bad (ecologically) has come from the medicinal and agrarian merging of practices, much good (medicinally, socially) has come from the shared human interest in plants. There are well known healing herbs of our folklore like lavender, St. John's Wort, peppermint, sassafras, nettle, High John the Conqueror, garlic and snakeroot that all had well known medical applications in addition to anti-witching associations.

And, there were well known witching herbs; ones that could magically locate water and minerals like witch-hazels and maples, there were one's who were sacred to fairies and devils like elder and willow, and plants that could be used to conjure victims; bryony, mandrake, shame-weed,[125] periwinkle, and bindweed. There were some pretty fascinating cross-cultural parallels where plants are concerned; trillium as a love charm on both coasts, person-shaped roots used for image-magic like the mandrake of the Old World and the bitterroot of the New, the oxalis root and species of rose used in love charms in European and Indigenous folk remedies.

The Doctrine of Signatures played a crucial role in herbal folk remedies in the New World and were the common cause for much folklore themselves. In fact, one thing shared amongst all the early herbal lore of most cultures is the perception of plants and their attributes as being indicative of their medicinal or spiritual use, and who better would know the spirit of a thing than witches, people who were thought to be well-versed in the hidden knowledge of spirited things.

A heart-shaped herb, when worn, will soften the hearts of those around you,[126] a ten-fingered leaf would control the one you love - the power of likeness is a defining feature of magical folk herbalism. *The Doctrine of Signatures* is integral to American folk herbal medicine and magical practices, a philosophy that continues today. This tradition of assigning uses to plants based on their physical qualities has less to do with medicine and more to do with magic, but still, we regard the American pharmacopoeia as a multicultural and intercontinental information exchange that further serves to highlight the parallels between cultures and their beliefs, especially as they converge in the New World.

Among the plants we associate with practitioners of magic and their work in the Americas are:

- *Apples and Cherries - The* New World had cherry trees before our European ancestors brought the apples we all know and love as part of the symbolism of the United States, but both became standard ingredients in love projects and witchlore itself. We all know the stories of poison apples and apples of evil, but they are also portents of love, omens of marriage, mediums between us and the spirit world. Most popular at the sabbat times, apple magic was absorbed into the general folklore of America from Western European folk charms and has become a uniquely American tradition of love fortunes, water-witching, and folk medicinal lore.

- *High John* - this member of the *ipomoea* is a plant with a personality; a spirit[127] that inhabits each root. Regularly identified and substituted (depending on the informant) with Solomon Seal and St John's Wort; it is by far the most popular in hoodoo, conjure, rootwork and other Afro American magical traditions and has a fascinating set of regional legends and African American folk tales[128] illustrating its cultural association with magic and use among all kinds of magical practitioners. It's value for protection and prosperity also included protection from the ill luck caused by witchery.

- *Low John or Trillium* - In Southern hoodoo this is known as low John or bethroot and grows as a lovely white flower with roots whose power is associated with love and luck. In Pacific Northwest herbal folk medicine, trillium bulb was used in love and beauty charms.[129]

- *Garlic* - the same garlic utilized in Pennsylvania German American folk magical anti-witch charms[130] is the same garlic reportedly used among Southwest natives as a protective charm.[131] Anecdotally; garlic wreaths were a protective kitchen ornament against the Devil in my household, and in many other homes in Southern California. Southwestern kitchens in general of all ethnic backgrounds sometimes keep garlic and pepper wreaths as symbols, storage, decor and yes, even folk magic.

- *Red Pepper* - used for anti-witching purposes, protective charms and even some love charms among both Indigenous and African Americans[132] eventually absorbed into general

American folklore as a protective and anti-witch charm (red-pepper tossed into a witch's skin would prevent her from flying home according to the Brown collection (p.117).

- *Angelica* - few other herbs are as important in American hoodoo and conjure than this root, and it has long been regarded in the English medicinal pharmacopoeia as a beneficial healing herb - regarded by Culpeper as a cure for fevers, and in the Americas, was used for the curing of witch-caused ailments.[133]

- *Willow* - used in traditional medicine around the world as a pain reliever, the willow also holds funereal folklore in the Northeast where it is associated with death and cemeteries. The Willow in American folk magic is often associated with death and sorrow, and in the Old World, they were occasionally associated with the Devil and witchcraft.

- *Bloodroot (sanguinaria canadensis)* - introduced to hoodoo from Indigenous American folk medicine,[134] this root has extensive use in prosperity and protective spells in different magical traditions of the Americas.

- *Mandrake, Bitterroot and Bryony* - these roots being used in the production of all manner of amulet, those of; love, beauty, sex, necromancy, protection, conjure and hexing. Typically, these herbs of love are also the very same used in image magic in the way of a poppet or dolly. Mandrakes are not indigenous to the New World and don't grow in many places easily, so they are substituted for with bitterroot, dandelion, bryony root among others.

- *Rose* - The rose is the beloved symbolic flower of the States and by far one of the most prolific magical herbs of the international witching pharmacopoeia. A common traditional cosmetic additive in China, a symbol of death or silence in Rome, and, during the Victorian era in Britain and America (though a deeply religious time) the red rose was granted the highest esteem as the floral symbol of love in the *Language of Flowers*. The rose as it has spread across the world in its various forms has a universal meaning of love, beauty and power as well as divination (used in love prediction fortune spells). Wild rose appears as an anti-evil and anti-witchcraft charm in ethnobotanical lore of the Pacific Northwest (Turner) and an additive to love and protection spells of Western Europe. Today, the rose is a standard herbal addition to any love-related spell, especially in America where the rose and its colors hold symbolic meaning, in part due to the rose's association in traditional American tattoo art with loyalty and sacrifice as well as the continuing commercialization of floral language on St. Valentine's Day.

- *Snakeroots* (various) - The poison snake bite was almost always deadly in the old days, but roots with curative properties presented the opportunity to undo this harm; these were (in the South and Midwest) called 'snakeroots' which are six or so species of herbs with purported snake-bite curative properties. Snakeroots were absorbed into Afro American folk medicine and spirituality from the Northeast Indigenous tribes familiar with snakeroot medicine.

- *St. John's Wort* - some American folklore of the South claims that witches go hunting for this flower each year in its season while other lore says this plant drives witches away but all folklore in the Americas generally regard this herb as highly medicinal in numerous aspects while also keeping the evils of witches, demons and fairies at bay. The folkloric and medicinal significance of this herb was introduced to us from Western European settlers. St. Johns and High John are commonly conflated in old folklore, but the two couldn't be more different.

- *Sassafras* - this herb was a mighty cure-all well-loved in the South. It appears throughout folkloric collections as a medication for rheumatism,[135] anti-witch charm[136] which could break charms in combination with fire, and as a general folk medicinal component.

- *Southernwood* - Introduced to New York and New England around the 1700's from Western Europe, quickly spread to Massachusetts folk charms and folklore. Being aromatic, it was used to disguise bad smells in the Old World and was also used in funeral bouquets in England. It was also used as a pest repellant; to drive away moths and protect clothing. Primary folk magical uses; love fortunes, divination games, and charms; anti-witching as well as bewitching, hex projects, aphrodisiac, attraction, drawing and guarding love.[137] Medicinally used as a wash for skin blemishes, as an antiseptic as well as a stimulant, aphrodisiac (which leached into its folk magic). Implemented through teas and potions; the whole herb was carried as a talisman, or in pillow charms (these being shared by both German and African American folk magic), and in shoes. The majority of our Southernwood folklore is found in the *Journal of American folklore*, Emrich Collection and *Memoirs of American Folk Society* (as well as in books of New English folktales like that of Alice Morse Earle*).

- *Jimsonweed (Thornapple)* - also called moonflower or devil's snare; this family of witching root holds a place of association with the flying ointment folklore of the Old World. In the New, this plant (the *stramonium* and *innoxia* species) was used by various Eastern, Southwestern, Mexican and South American peoples in spiritual ceremony. Jimson Weed is a pan-cultural magical substance and is used in conjure work to bring harm[138] or love, just as it was used in Europe and Indigenous America for similar or parallel purposes. Today, witches the world

over connect in a kind of international gardening cult of
datura growing witches.

These herbs of witching are just some of the more well-known of
the New World pharmacopoeia, but plant medicine and magic
doesn't operate by the rules of popularity. It's more important
to know your own bioregion, to learn about the plants and
their powers of where you work and live. Witchcraft isn't about
copying all the old formulas and spells today, it's about being
resourceful with what you have, so appreciate the plants around
you. Many of the traditional witching herbs have counterparts
that can be used for substitution. Be explorative, be creative, and
most importantly, be mindful of these powerful green spirits
and their medicine. Plants can be dangerous, they can bewitch
and befoul you, it's not something to dabble in blindly, so take
are upon the green path of witchcraft...

The Green Path Home

Of course, witchcraft doesn't take place in the distant gardens
of other witches. It takes place in the world around us. The
witches of old, like shamans and cunning men, would have had
knowledge of the herbs, trees, minerals and natural phenomenon
around them. A witch would have worked with the land they
lived on and the spirits there on a daily basis. For those who
take an animistic folkloric path as a witch in this New World,
the most sacred place we know is the place in which we do our
work.

My animistic faith can be broadly applied but my practice
relies on the spiritual influences, plants and life sustained around
me where I've built my work. These days, bioregional animism
is the new rising star in the traditional witch community; taking
a deeper interest in one's personal environment and sustaining
a practice and even a tradition of magic within it, based on its
specific ecologically interconnected regional attributes.

The riverside magic in the shadow of the great god-mountain Takoma is where I make my work, it's the spirits that I know and the plant spirit medicine that builds my own personal pharmacopoeia. But then again, I was born and partially raised in Southern California, among a totally different landscape of herbs and folk medicine. In the dusty hillsides, in a community that was primarily Latin-American, mixed-Indigenous and African American, the folk medicine of the people became accessible to my family through our relationships with people for whom the folk medicine of Latin America was basic life- - not magic; it was just life. There, the medicine of aloes is all-too-well known for those burns, and my *tia* always taught us to grow your peas, beans and squash together. Sage smoke and hemp tea; corn silk for stomach aches and the fragrance of all the many fruits of the earth baking in the sunshine - this was my first exposure to the green path. When we moved to the Northwest, I spent more time with people connected to the Puget Sound on a cultural and spiritual level, and all this exposure to the land and the people who understood it on historical, familial, and educational levels shaped my perception of the important role that herbs and plants play in survival and preservation of people and their customs, their ways of life.

Based on both the folklore of my own ancestors and the local medicinal plant traditions of the coast I've built my own regional pharmacopoeia, my own plant knowledge of the place I work my folk medicine and magic. It is the green current of my tradition of New World witchcraft and it represents the sacred seat of my animistic faith. My love roots are trillium, huckleberry, bedstraw and vetch; my lucky herbs are tiger lily, devil's club and thistle. The witching roots of the Green River are false hellebores and red elderberries, and the anti-witching herbs of the deep wood is devil's club and wild rose. The roots of these plants were once used in the folk charms and medicine of the local people and continue their spirit-work today with we witches of the river.

The medicine is powerful, the respect I have is religious, social and cultural.

I know the nettles are delicious, but you've got to be careful when you pick them, and I know that cedar bark can make or cure *damn near* anything. I know that weaving cattail mats take skill and that the bramble needs to be dewormed before eating. The liberty caps of Lincoln Park, the amanita-birch trails in SeaTac, the skunk-cabbage-patches of Seahurst, the marsh-vetch of the Green River, the poison hemlock and yarrow stalks along the Duwamish riverside - in this great urban sprawl, there are practitioners who continue the tradition of herbal remedies for the mind, body and spirit in relation to the green land around them, to their most familiar of spirits.

I urge all New World witches to take pride in their own home and always strive to remember the inseparable interconnectivity, the fundamentally interwoven connections of the folk, their land and their magic. Find the magic of wayside herbs and weeds, of those trees in the parks and algae in the lakes. Be aware of your surroundings and draw power from that place and its many sources.

Chapter 8

Ancestral Challenges

Spirits at War

The neo-pagan experience creates some cognitive dissonance in spiritual regard for people of mixed descent. Am I supposed to only practice the magic of the people who *look* like me? What if I don't know where my ancestors came from past America? What if I wasn't raised within a singular "ethnic" group? Why should one of my grandmothers be worthy of honor while the other starves for my love? Why do I have to choose to be *one* thing just to fit in with *one* crowd? Why am I sometimes rejected for embracing and eclectic array of cultural concepts familiar to me? There are no easy answers here.

Not all mixed witches are comfortable with their multiracial identity. Even the term "mixed-raced" was culturally taboo until my lifetime. Admitting you were mixed was a historical no-no (especially if you were mixed with African). For some people, their ancestors were subjected to incredible injustice and there is a note of discord in the idea of worshiping the gods of the people who you are only related to through the rape, forced-breeding and theft of one of your grandparents. That's a pretty horrific spiritual trauma to reconcile and it's one that many black American witches will face while discovering the roots of their practice. There are too many complex layers surrounding "race" in this country to prescribe some sort of cure-all. No one can tell you which of your ancestors to reject or accept, and there are no right and wrong answers to this spiritual battle (if it's one you face).

There's never a simple answer to the questions left to us by the injustices of history. Practitioners need to decide for themselves what aspects of their ancestry and familial history they are comfortable with on a spiritual level. If racial connotations mean a lot to your religious perceptions and influence your spirituality, then you'll need to do a lot of soul searching and be secure with your choice.

The beautiful thing about American culture as a whole is that we are by our nature a multicultural experience; the folklore and legends, myths, customs and superstitions of the many have shaped us all. That doesn't mean we should walk in and welcome ourselves within any tradition of folk magic across the country; it means that there is a plethora of witchlore, folk magic, and occultism that has always been accessible to all Americans through our collective folkloric magical practices and broadly-spread superstitions, and it's okay to start at that baseline of syncretic folk beliefs rather than trying to reach for initiatory or insular magical traditions. Culturally insular traditions or initiatory covens are following a very specific formula, but the folkloric witchcraft of America is a broad pool of beliefs from which we source our work, and so we need to approach our path from the accessibility at our fingertips while respecting the cultural nuances and boundaries that run alongside our path.

Decoction or Dilution?

Sometimes the folk magical practices of an area are long diluted from whatever origin they began in. *Brujeria* today doesn't look like folk Catholicism of the old days, and Southern cunning today doesn't look the way it did when communities were still more racially insular. The Voodoo of New Orleans today is a far cry from the Afro-diaspora tradition from which it emerged. In ways both cruel and kind, American folk magical beliefs and their traditions have become a thing accessible to the people, and this evolution of religion and spirituality is as natural as can be. In some ways, the evolution of syncretic spirituality illustrates the change we as a society endure constantly. In other ways, it also represents what can happen when coerced assimilation suppresses our society's component cultures. Much was lost in translation, including the cultural significance of some of the folk magical practices we see throughout our collections; this is a combination of poor research, misunderstandings of Indigenous religious practices, witch hysteria and the general conflation of religious beliefs of Africans and Natives as inferior and infernal in the eyes of the Christian European settlers.

The subject of cultural dilution is also a heavy one in the pagan community; when are we *honoring* our ancestry and when are we diluting the cultural significance of the practices we take up? This is another hard question without a clear answer. There can be some clear-cut instances of people benefiting from the authentic sacred spiritual practices of a specific culture without any context and education; a mishmash of Indigenous American ceremonies, Indian religious decoration, Hoodoo plant rituals and new-age goddess philosophy masquerading as a new ceremony... this is the kind of problematic behavior that attracts controversy.

Context is key, education about the cultures from which you have derived spiritual lessons is a component to authenticity. Teaching profit-based classes and courses which combine the sacred ceremonies of unrelated cultures and spiritualities and failing to properly attribute where these are coming from is a problem. Picking out a "cool" aspect of a foreign spirituality and marketing this as your own is bound to raise eyebrows because it fails to address the fact that these ceremonies are being extracted from communities that are largely marginalized and underrepresented.

In America, it is an especially sensitive subject and the context of our history plays a role in the sensitivities many Americans have when they see people in a position of power or majority exploiting aspects of cultures which have largely been harmed by those very actions. For some Americans, this kind of dilution harms the greater fabric of what makes us unique... and yet for other Americans, this sense of cultural egg-shell-stepping feels like gatekeeping, maybe even bigotry - an attack on their freedoms to associate with whatever they want. My intention isn't to argue the morality but to highlight that the multicultural experience of America's magical traditions is more complicated than the surface level. This is a nuanced issue, one that challenges our preconceived notions of culture and identity and there is no room to compartmentalize this particular social issue, as it is intersectional with so many others. When we approach magic in this country, we are also approaching people's cultures and their identities, and we need to be mindful of that.

There's also the matter of how magic *outside* of witchcraft affects America's relationship with magic. The non-witchcraft folk-magical traditions of conjure, rootwork and hoodoo are all American traditions that developed from an effort to preserve West African religious systems during the transatlantic slave trade and after. Hoodoo, like conjure, developed in part as a resistance tool, a tool against oppression and oppressors, and this is intrinsically tied to the identities of many witches of color in the States. For practitioners of African American spirituality, these practices are tied to their ancestral identity, to the survival of who they are at the core, and some may perceive the practice as being "lessened" by being diluted with non-African American influences; a sort of disservice to their mission and their faith.

African American folk magical traditions are complicated; there are some traditions that are deeply reflective of West African spirituality preserved, and there are traditions, like conjure, which are comprised of West African spiritual structures, folk magical Christianity of Europe and Indigenous folk medicine and folk narrative elements. Conjure as a whole is a syncretic set of religious traditions that is inseparable from its West African elements, and for some practitioners of color, this is a point of sensitivity. For some black American practitioners, the magic at their disposal and within their practice comes from the era of necessity, where you use what you've got to get what you need, to defend yourself from spiritual and physical oppression. I won't make a judgment as to what is right or wrong - that's not my place in this work. What I will say, as an American of color, is that this is a sensitive minefield that needs to be approached with respect and regard to context. Racial history in the USA is too bloody and traumatic to warrant being minimized or negated. When approaching spiritualities tied to other people's cultures, do so with the utmost understanding that your own perspective on this culture is not the reality. You may not agree with what you hear or see, but you will have at least learned to listen and that needs to be a start. I firmly believe this applies to all people; approach any space with respect and open ears and you will avoid unnecessary drama, and always pay attribution to the people and history you are representing.

As we move forward with embracing multiculturality, we cannot mistake multiculturality for *unlimited* access. We cannot mistake *inclusion* for *appropriation*. The broader American culture to which we all belong already allows us to represent the spectrum of folk magic in our work without undermining the spiritual ceremonies of specific cultures or communities. We share enough cross-culturally to bond over what we have in common than over what we do *not*. Be mindful, and be willing to educate yourself beyond books and media. Get some perspective from members of the spiritual communities that have influenced your practice and learn where your boundaries are.

We are a nation built from displacement, theft, persecution, immigration and assimilation; that we would fashion new traditions from old was bound to have its controversy. We're not attempting to lessen the traditions of our various ancestors by continuing with our syncretic practices; we're keeping the traditions we know and understand alive in our own way, by our own complex cultural standards. What we have here isn't pure, it isn't a direct lineage from some older tradition. What we have here is 400 years of multiculturality, and that is as pure to **us** as we can get. If one is interested in pursuing a "pure" cultural tradition of folk religion, you won't find it easily in America, and if you do, best of luck.

We as modern witches have a moral obligation to be conscientious of our practices as derivative of other, older, culturally specific practices, and we need to respect that there is a boundary between the syncretic folk magical systems American people and the cultural-religious customs that influenced them. By doing so, we claim our own heritage rather than someone else's. We also have an opportunity to celebrate the home-grown and syncretic traditions of our regions and our migration between them, that crossing of roads is where witches are meant to gather anyway.

Move forward carefully when approaching witchcraft and magic itself from the angle of a single culture rather than from our *general* culture, this is a territory of emotional and historical landmines. If you are looking towards rootwork, hoodoo and conjure, or powwow, or *brujeria*, approach this with the racial and cultural context in mind and with regards and respect to the people who live in these traditions, who speak the lingo and know the cosmology. Learn, understand and respect the boundaries you face if your pursuit takes you down one particular path.

There will always be a vocal minority who ignorantly assume the practices of marginalized people for the exotic trend of it, and those people also need to be corrected on the problematic nature of *appropriation*. There's a big difference between *appreciation* and *appropriation*, and there's a time for natural exchange and for treading lightly. The history of assimilation and conversion has created a kind of unique paradox when it comes to appropriation. It can be hard to know what is American culture, and what is cultural *within* America. When we walk into the spaces of marginalized cultures, we are approaching from a sensitive place dealing with the trauma of historical events and atrocities.

It's important to give credit where it's due, no matter who you're working with and to know who and what you are representing to the world; do so with the utmost respect as you go. Allow the space you are entering to welcome *you* and be ready to face some differences you may not be prepared to deal with. And for those opening their cultural-spiritual communities to those *outside* of it, do so with patience, I beg you, to change this world and the people in it by allowing the space to unlearn, to misstep and to relearn.

There are a lot of different cultures that make up America, and some of those are overly-exhausted communities who are susceptible to regular culture theft while being offered nothing in return. It can wound people and it's worth it for us as Americans to regard the kinship between us with some empathy. We may never agree on what's right and wrong, but having a conversation about it in the first place is the only way we've ever made things work.

Mixed in the Middle

Americans have a complicated relationship with racial and cultural conversations. We oscillate between discomfort at confronting the reality, and confrontational behavior when we *do*. It pervades all aspects of the racial conversation and is part of the dualistic divisiveness that has become part of our social/political order. Too often, the individual cultural experience is overlooked and masked behind shame, guilt, appropriation, identity politics and social stigmas. When we speak of the multiracial witch experience, what comes to mind? For me, the diversity of people and their beliefs IS the American experience. This is my life, my culture - it is how I perceive this country and what I believe makes this land exceptional.

The experiences of each American is unique and it's not always a simple matter of "race" and ethnicity. There are many

Americans who are not ethnically related to the predominant surrounding culture in which they are living. There are Americans who do not resemble the dominant culture to which they belong. There are people like me who pass for a multitude of ethnicities and are judged accordingly. There are people who are mixed with two or more different and distinct ethnicities and they live as part of both cultures, or part of neither. There are Americans who come from families where nobody looks like one another; where no one is a genetic relative and children are raised in a mentality of diversity and exposure and cultural exchange.

I'm from a family like that. Mine is a family where multiple languages are spoken in each household, everyone has different skin colors, most of us are related through some form of adoption, and most siblings share only one biological parent if any. We are one of those classic new-normal families and I'm determined to reach out to the others out there like me who know what it's like to live in different cultural and racial worlds. There are hundreds of different dynamics to culture and "race", and each experience is worth understanding because each one is part of the American experience. At those edges, where cultures and ethnicities and heritages and religions meet, there are people like me. There are millions of people of mixed descent, there are people living a multicultural identity, there are people living in-between worlds, and some of us are witches. Magic in the New World is unique because it no longer resembles the people who delivered this wisdom; it resembles a combination of human faith.

For some like myself, folk magic was such an intrinsic part of one's familial spirituality and cultural identity that there is no separating the two. My siblings and I were brought up placing pennies above our door, setting out spirit plates, drumming, honoring our ancestors and gods at various altars... We all have altars; my mom, my sister, some of my aunties. It isn't witchcraft for them. Only a few of us are witches - witchery is a younger generation phenomenon, but the altars they keep are magic nonetheless; some to the *orishas*, others to Mary and St. Lucy. My *tía's* altar back home in SoCal used to have these delicate and ornate porcelain *soperas*; a big golden one just for Oshun, with *lamparas* and fat yellow pumpkin flowers all around. Mom's altar is full of beautiful black Madonnas and crosses studded with *milagros*, and my sister's altars look similar, only with her many saints and Yemaja at the center. Auntie Lei's altar was a Haida ancestral altar with a traditional black and red button blanket and cedar woven hat... Uncle's altar used to have a massive buffalo skull (he's a Sioux boy) with all his regalia neatly placed beside - and there was *always* sweet-grass hanging nearby. I grew up smelling sage in one room, myrrh in another, sweet-grass in the basement, copal in my room. Even my very Christian father had an "altar" to his ancestors as well as famous black musicians and civil rights leaders; his own way of honoring where he comes from.

Folk magical practices express themselves in all manner of religion, even those that espouse anti-magical beliefs, and because of that it can act as the background religion for some people. In some ways, this forms unique traditions within families; the one in my household even provided its own tutelary spirits, rules regarding silence, the dead, luck, protection and the like. These traditions may only be a few generations old but the impact it's had on my siblings and I was unifying and connective despite us holding different religious affiliations.

There are folk medicinal charms and magical practices absorbed from sources, some of which I don't even know and some that are as common as dirt. I suspect there are a lot of families who actually have their own traditions of magical-spiritual practices; after all, folklore is largely hereditary - being passed down from generation to generation within families, communities, towns...

My idea of magic was shaped by my cultural understandings, and those understandings were formed under entirely different circumstances than yours, then others. That doesn't make me right, or wrong, it makes me unique and frankly, I'd rather be that than some carbon-copy of another person's idea of a good American witch. Maybe being mixed is a dishonor to some people, maybe honoring all of my ancestors sickens bigots and riles militants and pisses off prejudice people. I certainly hope so. It satisfies me to know I've done my civic American duty and pissed off a supremacist or two. My ancestors are proud of me, and it's them I look to for guidance.

Chapter 9

Forging a New Path

At the Crossroads

How does one even go about forging ahead with a sense of tradition out of the intangibility of it all? Some people found their own traditions based on their unique practice and share this with other like-minded people, or, one could attempt to associate with more formalized traditions like those of Voodoo, hoodoo or conjure, Santeria, obeah or granny magic - but that means you need to make contacts in that community, undergo training and initiation into their mysteries, work within that framework. It's a long and difficult road and the nature of mysticism is secrecy and silence, so finding formal traditions to adopt into can be exceedingly difficult. Not to mention the fact that not all witches are looking to find community in a bound circle or church or organization.

Most folk witches throughout history would not have actually belonged to austere secret societies with elaborate ceremonial rituals and lengthy rules and initiations. A witch was simply a person who took up the forbidden arts, a layperson of any kind. The "traditions" to which they belonged were more often than not, informal. Let's be real; witchcraft isn't about a revealed tradition with a long and unbroken lineage.

Real witchcraft is dirty, gritty, highly individualistic and is about using what one has at their disposal to make their will be done. If your heart really is in a formalized practice where you follow a specific set of instructions on how to be a certain kind of witch in a certain kind of ideology, then more power to you. Fact is, that formality doesn't lend to legitimacy. Having a long lineage means nothing - to be clear; most popular Western traditions we know of, from Thelema to Wicca to Tubal Cain were all operating on knowledge revealed to them through *gnosis*, supported by multiple literary, historical and spiritual sources and put into a formalized practice, but they weren't unbroken lineages of witchcraft stretching through the ages; they were revealed wisdom.

Because of famed formalized traditions, there is a pervasive culture of gatekeeping when it comes to what is and is not "traditional". The formal traditions of witchcraft and magic as we know it are recent creations which evolved from a litany of sources, and there's absolutely nothing wrong with that, it simply is one road to take, but it isn't at all necessary. Witchcraft is the spirituality of the layperson, so no formality is needed when your sole duty is to use that which is at your disposal to exert your will. Folk magic most of all is the craft of the common folk, accessible to all.

So, if we're looking to construct more formalized currents of witchcraft from the traditional witchcraft found in American folklore and spirituality, one place we can begin to look is from the cultural perspective. I've written pretty extensively enough about how the regions of America are defined by the Indigenous group and the settling cultures which converged there, and witchcraft and magic in a region of America are also defined by what cultures settled there. If most traditions of magical practice in America arose from the combined supernatural and superstitious beliefs of the common people, and those common people, for the most part, agreed that the world was inhabited by those with the powers of witchcraft, then it stands to reason that the incredible exchange of folk magical practices (anti-witch charms, chap-books, and occult pamphlets) isn't simply a matter of *theft*, there's an element of necessity at play.

Turning to local **folklore** is the best place to start, as well as the folklore of your ancestors and of those cultures which have shaped your worldview. If the traditions of a region rather than a specific cultural group appeal to you, this could be one method of forging ahead with your own tradition of magic. Get to know your area. Know the genius loci and folk-figures, the local haunts and their kinds spirit, the wells of power and the places where witches gather.

Understand the people who built your area and get to know the magic, the plants, animals, minerals and whether of your home. Acquaint yourself with the history and the spirit of the place where you do your craft. Don't look too high up and too far away for the spirits and their wisdom, or you'll miss what's right in front of you. Start with your family and your known ancestry and work out from there. Often times, Americans know more about where in the country their people came from than what country they immigrated from, and since the communities of America are largely reflective of the population that settled there (Germans of Pennsylvania, Gullahs of South Carolina for example), we're able to get a small view of where or folklore comes from and who may have generated it.

Many multiracial pagans will identify with the naturally eclectic practice of regional folkloric witchcraft which can be a comfortable foundation in which we can express our spiritual and magical diversity. The general folklore of the Americas has rather innocuous cultural connotations at this point and reflects the collection of magical knowledge of the whole land. It is specific to our culture as North Americans and reflects the regions of the land and the influences of the people there, and is accessible for us to explore.

Other witches may want to follow a *specific* cultural tradition of magic like voodoo or pow-wow, or certain sects of conjure and hoodoo (often, these are societies with initiatory structure); these are still syncretic American systems but they're better learned in-person, where the seeker is being taught within the context of the culture to which this folk magic derives. Immersion into a culture when learning their traditions is a respectful way to appreciate without appropriating and allows you to shed your preconceived notions for first-hand experience. These established traditions can greatly influence the path of your own making and give you an opportunity to respect the people who are sharing their spirituality with you.

Our heritage as a country opens doorways between people, and the folkloric heritage of America is by its nature one that is shared across cultural and color lines. There's a difference between practicing folk magic and practicing an established tradition - the point is not to pick and choose from multiple sources and pass it off as an authentically American witchcraft tradition. The point ought to be to understand the foundations of our folklore, their origins, and respect the role they play in our shared culture.

Folk magical practices in America are intersectional; the threads of our traditions stretch across the country, moving and expanding just as our ancestors and us tend to move and expand. They cross over regions and States and connect distant people, places, and beliefs. It is from these points of synthesis that witches like myself get an understanding of the mutual beliefs shared between our ancestors. An American folk-witch has an opportunity to connect at this hub of spiritual transmission: connect to their ancestors, connect to their land, connect to their country as a whole. And for multiracial and multicultural witches, all of us out there, this is a place of connection to everyone who made us what we are.

Exploring and Collecting Traditions

When taking the traditional and folkloric path, nothing will be more valuable to you than oral traditions from prime resources and literary collections. County libraries and college libraries tend to have fairly good collections of folklore both local and national; these will be invaluable resources when tracing the origin of the charms, tricks, and incantations you're sure to encounter in your exploration.

Universities and large libraries often have archives that you can access with the right credentials; often academic or student passes are required but that varies. State history museums tend to capture aspects of folk-life that include folklore and superstitions and can be a fun exploration of what people were thinking when they developed their folktales. Ethnographies and spiritual texts, poetry books and children's rhymes; all these facets of society captured in the written word contain information on how people viewed the spiritual and magical world around them and how the mystic has influenced their cultures and lives - and ours. The fact is the study of folk magic also entails the study of history, religion and society.

Get involved with local folklore societies and cultural community centers if you want to learn about the people around you and their superstitions and folk-ways. Gather stories from people with more experience than yourself - your elders, and never underestimate the education you can find in the strange and rare literature you come across. Most of all, follow your intuition; you'll find what feels right to you often matches up with the successes in your practice and you'll find that not all the old crafts are meant to evolve in this new era of folk magic.

When it comes to looking for the common threads between people's magical traditions, I find that it's easiest to research wide and far, narrow down the commonalities between the different magical traditions of each of *my* cultures and work from there. A familiar place is a stepping-stone to tracing your roots. Start with what you know about yourself, your family, your area and work from there. Gather knowledge from your immediate vicinity and untangle the roots as they go. This is where being mixed has a real benefit in *my* life; I've acquired this incredible gift of access to understanding all kinds of very different people just by embracing who I am and the people who raised me.

In My Crucible

Personally, what I know of witchery is extensively Americanized folklore - not purely reflective of the Old World but reflective of the post-Colonial synchronization of occult and mystical beliefs held by the average every-day American as we migrated throughout the country. The tradition of witchcraft I define as my *own* is one built specifically from the collective early herbal folklore of my West African, Southeastern Indigenous American and Western European ancestors - particularly during their periods of deep spiritual synchronicity as the cultures were blending heavily together in the post-Colonial era. The place at which all my ancestors converged was in the realm of the plants. Whatever differences they had culturally, their combined folk herbal knowledge became the basis for the pharmacopeia of the United States, and the structure by which traditional medicine operated for my ancestor's aids in my understanding of the spiritual relationships within animism itself.

Plants and their powers were as deeply rooted in superstition and medicine for my ancestors enslaved in the Carolinas as it was to my impoverished ancestors in rural Florida. Plant spirits are so intrinsic to Indigenous spiritualities, particularly in my area of the country, that no ceremony takes place where sacred herbs are not present, and the local folklore of plants derived entirely from the traditions of the local tribes. Herbs and all their mysterious works are part of the spiritual and cultural foundations of *all* people who came to America and where these roads met, the traditional practices of these people changed thereafter.

The tradition that was formed between me and my companions represented the animistic, naturalistic and folkloric nature of American regional witchcraft as we saw it; our bioregional animism, our sense of multiracial identity, our folkloric spiritualities. By combining spiritual ecology, animistic faith with the folk-magic of our ancestors, we are best able to serve the spirits and our ancestors and the land itself.

From there, the *Crucibulum* Tradition was forged (or rather, *began* forging) and we began carving out our own niche in the fabric of magic in our part of the world. The name was chosen as a nod to Miller's masterpiece of American social commentary as well as a reference to the "melting pot" so many of us grew up with (despite the new politically correct lingo). For us, a combination of witches, pagans, alchemists and mystics, the *Crucibulum* became a fabulous salon where occult philosophy and cultural expression could be freely discussed and shared without restraint. Animism, nature and ancestor veneration, agrarian and funereal customs and folkloric magic are the foundations of the tradition I work within, something I share with many practitioners around me. *The Crucibulum* allowed for all of us involved in its creation to express our own cultural identity under a unified practice, one that transcends color and culture lines and goes straight to the heart of the country: the folk.

All of our ancestors delivered unto this land their folklore regarding nature spirits, natural functions, appeasing spirits, banishing them, helping the land to grow, helping life to end, charms for love and ways to read the future. From the older sources of folklore, story-telling, tall-tales, and local legends, I extract the formulas and models that appeal to my spirituality and apply them in a modern way; in service to the land and the bones.

A Final Word

Today, our values, morals, ideologies, and philosophies have deeply evolved, globally affected. We need to be comfortable with traditional witchcraft as we know it in the New World, where we are influenced by all aspects of the Western Magical Traditions, where our own unique folklore reflects and occult diversity of beliefs that transcends racial and cultural boundaries and permeate the general folk magical mind of our country. The traditions we build now will influence the future, and I hope whatever we do, we keep alive these old ways.

Folkloric and traditional witchcraft in America has some growing up to do, some evolving. We've got to define what witchcraft is for ourselves and I look forward to the conversation. Some people define traditional witchcraft in some very strict terms as:

A) British and British descended lineages of witchcraft tradition,

B) culturally-specific traditions of magical practice that parallel the European concept of witchcraft,

C) familial and/or community magical traditions or,

D) as *The Watkins Dictionary of Magic* defines it; *"a folk religion that blended with superstition, fortune-telling, folklore, and herbalism with remnants of various pre-Christian religion beliefs (e.g. Celts and Druids)."*

Like all things in the world, the very idea of tradition and witchcraft is diverse. My desire in this work is not to debate what traditional witchcraft is or is not; I've already defined it for myself and that's good enough for me. My desire is to highlight the diversity of thought surrounding the occult arts and to offer perspectives that can benefit our work as American witches. This is an opportunity for us to connect and converse about the magic between people.

We need to have deeper, broader conversations about what witchcraft means to our culture today now that we know well what it meant to our ancestors. We folkloric witches, New World witches, traditional American witches have an opportunity to define ourselves because we have the liberty to do so. To my fellow New World Witches, I offer you this reminder of ancient wisdom; *know thyself.* And to my fellow practitioners who identify as multicultural, multiethnic and/or multiracial, I urge you to *see yourself* in the reflection of our folk magic because you *are* reflected in it. We who are descended from the meeting of paths, here at the crossroads of cultures, in the crucible of cultural coalescence; we are at liberty to define the path we take in this New World, to make space for our ancestors and their sacred traditions. We here now, define the future of magic in America; all of us **together.**

Footnotes

1. Dorson, Richard M. *Buying the Wind: Regional Folklore in the United States: Mother Hicks the Witch*, 1964, (p.57)
2. Dalton, Michael *The Country Justice*, 1618
3. Hartlieb, Johannes *The Book of All Forbidden Arts, Superstition, and Sorcery*, 1475
4. Michelet, Jules; Allinson, Alfred Richard *The Sorceress*, 1939 edition, (p.89)
5. Wilby, Emma *Cunning Folk and Familiar Spirits: Shamanic Visionary Traditions in Early Modern British Witchcraft and Magic*, 2005, (p.42)
6. Godbeer, Richard *The Devil's Dominion: Magic and Religion in Early New England*, 1994, (p.158)
7. Games, Alison *Witchcraft in Early North America*, 2010, (p.3)
8. Simmons, Marc *Witchcraft in the Southwest: Spanish and Indian Supernaturalism on the Rio Grande*, 1980, (p.54)
9. *Journal of American Folklore Vol XXVII*, American Folk-lore Society, 1914, (p.328)
10. Cross, Tom Peete *Witchcraft in North Carolina*, 2015 Andesite Press reproduction edition (p.34)
11. [Simmons (p.57,58)]
12. Weisman, Richard *Witchcraft, Magic, and Religion in 17th-century Massachusetts*, 1984 (p.41)
13. Sullivan, Nancy *A Treasury of American Folklore: Our Customs, Beliefs, and Traditions*, 1994, (p.196)
14. [Games, (p.33)]
15. Chireau, Yvonne P. *Black Magic: Religion and the African American Conjuring Tradition*, 2006, (p.84)
16. Anderson, Jeffrey E. *Conjure in African American Society*, 2005, (p.53)
17. [Weisman (p.41)
18. Feest, Christian F. *Indians of Northeastern North America*,

1986, (p.16)

19. Cave, Alfred *Indian Shamans and* English, 1992, (p.24-26)

20. [Simmons, (p.107)]

21. Kilpatrick, Alan *The Night Has a Naked Soul: Witchcraft and Sorcery among the Western Cherokee,* 1998, (p.42)

22. Buerge, David M. *Roots and Branches: The Religious Heritage of Washington State,* 1988, (p.9)

23. Tingle, Tim *Spirits Dark and Light: Supernatural Tales from the Five Civilized Tribes,* 2006, (p.146)

24. Breslaw, Elaine G. *Witches of the Atlantic World* (2000): Parrinder, Geoffrey: *Witchcraft: European and African,* 1958, (p.145-146)

25. [Games, (p.20)]

26. [Chireau, (p.84]

27. White, Thomas *Witches of Pennsylvania: Occult History and Lore,* 2013

28. [Godbeer, (p.30)]

29. Piersen, William D. *Black Yankees: The Development of an Afro-American Subculture in Eighteenth-century New England,* 1988, (p.96)

30. Mather, Cotton *On Witchcraft,* 1692

31. [Anderson, (p.62)]

32. [Games, (p.6)]

332. [Anderson, (p.53)]

34. Torres, Eliseo "Cheo" *Healing with Herbs and Rituals: A Mexican Tradition,* (p.85)

35. Canizares, Raul J. *Cuban Santeria: Walking with the Night,* 1999

36. [Simmons, (p.107)]

37. Brown, Frank C. *The Frank C. Brown Collection of North Carolina Folklore Vol VII,* (p.112)

38. [Cross, (p.13)]

39. Daniels, Cora L. *Encyclopedia of Superstitions, Folklore and the Occult Sciences of the Word Vol II,* 1910, (p.862)

40. [Chireau (p.85,86)]
41. [Cross, (p.17)]
42. Aurand Jr., Ammon Monroe *The Realness of Witchcraft in America*, 1942, (p.11)
43. [Green, (p.166)]
44. Ginzburg, Carlo *Night Battles: Witchcraft and Agrarian Cults in the Sixteenth and Seventeenth Centuries*,1966, (p.43)
45. Green, Thomas A. *Latino American Folktale*, 2009, (p.165)
46. Botkin, B.A *A Treasury of Southern Folklore*, 1949, (p.541)
47. Chase, Richard *American Folk Tales and Songs*, 1956, (p.69)
48. Gainer, Patrick W. *Witches, Ghosts, and Signs, Folklore of the Southern Appalachians*, 2008, kindle edition
49. [Cross, (p.27)]
50. [FCB Vol VII, p.110]
51. Goss, Linda; Barnes, Marian *Talk That Talk: An Anthology of African-American Storytelling: Faulkner's The Ways of a Witch*, 1989, (p.307-310)
52. Randolph, Vance *Ozark Witchcraft and Folklore*, 1947, (p.267)
53. [FCB, Vol VII, (p.112)
54. Davis, Hubert J. *The Silver Bullet, and Other American Witch Stories*, 1975, (p.97)
55. Boatright, Mody Coggin; Mathis, Wilson *The Best of Texas Folk and Folklore*, 1916-1954, (p.253)
56. Prahlad, Anand *African American Folklore: An Encyclopedia for Students: An Encyclopedia for Students*, 2016, (p.31)
57. Sanders, Lynn Moss *Howard W. Odum's Folklore Odyssey: Transformation to Tolerance Through African American Folk Studies*, 2003, (p.70)
58. [FCB, Vol VII, (p.169)]
59. [Anderson, (p.61,62)]
60. [Aurand Jr., (p.14)]
61. [FCB, Vol VII, (p.136)]
62. [Daniels, CL, Vol I, (p.447)]
63. Gates, Henry Louis; Tatar, Maria *The Annotated African*

American Folktales, 2017, (p.232)

64. Barrie, Alexander *Sutton Companion to the Folklore, Myths and Customs of Britain*, 2005, (p.395)

65. Wehmeyer, Stephen C. *From the Back of the Mirror: "Quicksilver," Tinfoil, and the Shimmer of Sorcery in African-American Vernacular Magic: Magic, Ritual, and Witchcraft, Vol. 12 no. 2*, 2017, (p.163-185)

66. Emrich, Duncan *Folklore on the American Land*, 1972

67. Espinosa, Aurelio M. *The Folklore of Spain in the American Southwest: Traditional Spanish Folk Literature in Northern New Mexico and Southern Colorado*, 1990, (p.75)

68. Baker, Ronald L. *Hoosier Folk Legends*,1982, (p.9)

69. [Gainer, 2008, kindle edition]

70. [Botkin, (p.541)]

71. Hoffman, John George *Pow-Wows or, Long Lost Friend*, 1929, (p.61)

72. Milnes, Gerald *Signs, Cures, and Witchery: German Appalachian Folklore*, 2007, (p.168)

73. *Journal of American Folklore Vol XXVII*, 1914, (p.328)

74. [Anderson, (p.53)]

75. [Daniels, CL, Vol III, (p.1447)]

76. [Botkin, (p.634)]

77. Davies, Owen *America Bewitched: The Story of Witchcraft After Salem*, 2013, (p.34)

78. [Anderson, (p.71, 72)]

79. [Davies, (p.41-42)]

80. [Cross, (p.41)]

81. Prahlad, Anand *The Greenwood Encyclopedia of African American Folklore*, 2005, (p.636)

82. [Botkin, (p.663)

83. Brunvand, Jan Harold *American Folklore: An Encyclopedia*, 2006, (p.747)

84. Kelly, Ruth Edna, *The Book of Halloween*, 1919, (p.117)

85. Dickerson Bergen, Fanny; Newell, William Wells *Current*

Superstitions: Collected from the Oral Tradition of English Speaking Folk, 1896, (p.54)

86. [FCB VOL VI, (p.626)]
87. *Memoirs of the American Folk-lore Society*, 1896, (p.57)
88. [Cross, (p.18)]
89. Booth, Sally Smith, *The Witches of Early America*, 1975, (p.56)
90. [Kilpatrick, (p.8)]
91. [Botkin, (p.543-545)]
92. Hand, Wayland D. *Popular Beliefs and Superstitions from North Carolina*, 1964, (p.118)
93. Young, William Henry *Buy a Broom Besom: The Story of a Broom*, 1976, (p.38)
94. [Cross, (p.250)]
95. *Journal of American Folklore Vol XXII*, 1909, (p.254)
96. *Journal of American Folklore Vol V*, 1892, (p.111)
97. [Simmons, (p.58)]
98. [Cross, (p.64)]
99. [Cross, (p.32-33)]
100. Indiana University Research Center for the Language Sciences *Indiana Folklore, Volumes 11-13*, 1978, (p.48)
101. Hole, Christina *A Mirror of Witchcraft*, 1957, (p.60)
102. [Sullivan/Hardin, (p.224)]
103. [Kilpatrick, (p.8)
104. [Booth, (p.34)]
105. [Sullivan/Hardin, (p.402)]
106. Müller-Ebeling, Claudia; Rätsch, Christian; Storl, Wolf-Dieter *Witchcraft Medicine: Healing Arts, Shamanic Practices, and Forbidden Plants*, 2003, (p.51)
107. Skinner, Charles M *Myths and Legends of Our Own Land Vol II*, 1896, (p.225-227)
108. Alexander, Skye *Mermaids: The Myths, Legends, and Lore*, 2012, (p.60)
109. Haase, Donald *The Greenwood Encyclopedia of Folktales and Fairy Tales*, 2007, (p.620)

110. [Simmons, (p.62)]

111. Turner, Nancy *Ancient Pathways, Ancestral Knowledge: Ethnobotany and Ecological Wisdom of Indigenous Peoples of Northwestern North America: Vol II*, 2014, (p.259)

112. [Booth, (p.34)

113. [FCB Vol VII (p.395)]

114. [FCB Vol VII (p.394-396)]

115. Martin, Laura C. *The Folklore of Birds*, 1996, (p.93)

116. Cohn, Norman *Europe's Inner Demons: An Enquiry Inspired by the Great Witch Hunt*, 1975, (p.228)

117. Gunther, Erna *Ethnobotany of Western Washington*, 1973, (p.26)

118. [Turner Vol I, p.458)]

119. Wadsworth, Thomson *The Aztecs of Central Mexico: An Imperial Society*, 2005

120. Adams Jr., James D.; Garcia, Cecilia; Lien Eric J. *A Comparison of Chinese and American Indian (Chumash) Medicine*, 2007

121. Mokgobi, M.G, *Understanding Traditional African Healing*, 2014

122. [Games, (p.19)]

123. Lee, Michele Elizabeth *Working the Roots: Over 400 Years of Traditional African American Healing*, 2017

124. [Torres, (p.14)]

125. [Botkin, (p.633)]

126. Burton, Thomas G.; Manning, Ambrose N. *A Collection of Folklore by Undergraduate Students of East Tennessee State University*, 1966, (p.88)

127. [Prahlad, (p.712)]

128. Cohn, Amy *From Sea to Shining Sea: A Treasury of American Folklore and Folk Songs*, 1993, (p.134,135)

129. [Gunther, (p.26)]

130. [Aurand, (p.14)]

131. [Simmons (p.147-8)]

132. [Anderson, (p.80)]

133. [Davies, (p.27)]

134. [Anderson, (p.80)]

135. [FCB Vol VI, (p.236)]

136. [Burton, Manning, (p.47)]

137. Emrich, Duncan *The Folklore of Love and Courtship: The Charms and Divinations, Superstitions and Beliefs, Signs and Prospects of Love, Sweet Love,*1970, (p.47)

138. [Anderson, (p.68)]

Sources

Adams, Jr, James D.; Garcia, Cecilia; Lien, Eric J. *A Comparison of Chinese and American Indian (Chumash) Medicine: Abstract,* 2008, Evidence-Based Complementary and Alternative Medicine Volume 7, Issue 2, Pages 219-225

Anderson, Jeffrey E. *Conjure in African American Society,* LSU Press, 2008

Aurand, Ammon Monroe *The Realness of Witchcraft in America: Witch-doctors, Apparitions, Pow-wows, Heserei, Angels, Devils, Hex, Sex: Witches or No Witches, You Should Read this Account,* Aurand Press, 1942

Baker, Ronald L. *Hoosier Folk Legends,* Indiana University Press, 1982

Barrie, Alexander *Sutton Companion to the Folklore, Myths and Customs of Britain,* History Press, 2005

Boatright, Mody C.; Hudson, Wilson; Maxwell, Allen *The Best of Texas Folk and Folklore, 1916-1954,* University of North Texas Press, 1998

Booth, Sally Smith *The Witches of Early America,* Hastings House, 1975

Botkin, B.A *A Treasury of American Folklore,* Crown, 1944

Botkin, B.A *A Treasury of Southern Folklore,* Bonanza Books, 1949

Breslaw, Elaine G. *Witches of the Atlantic World: An Historical Reader and Primary Sourcebook,* NYU Press, 2000

Brown, Frank C.; White, Newman Ivey, Hand, Wayland D.; *The Frank C. Brown Collection of North Carolina Folklore in Seven Volumes,* Duke University Press, 1952-

Brunvand, Jan Harold *American Folklore: An Encyclopedia,* Routledge, 2006

Canizares, Raul J. *Cuban Santeria: Walking with the Night,* Inner Traditions/Bear, Mar 1, 1999

Cave, Alfred *Indian Shamans and English Witches,* Essex Institute

Historical Collections, 1992

Chase, Richard *American Folk Tales and Songs*, New American Library, 1956

Chireau, Yvonne P. *Black Magic: Religion and the African American Conjuring Tradition*, University of California Press, 2006

Cohn, Amy *From Sea to Shining Sea: A Treasury of American Folklore and Folk Songs*, Scholastic Inc., 1993

Cohn, Norman *Europe's Inner Demons: The Demonization of Christians in Medieval Christendom*, University of Chicago Press, 1993

Congdon, Kristin G. *Uncle Monday and Other Florida Tales*, Univ. Press of Mississippi, 2001

Cross, Tom Peete *Witchcraft in North Carolina; Volume XVI*, The University of North Carolina, Andesite Press reproduction edition, 2015, originally published 1919

Dalton, Michael *The Country Justice: Containing the Practice of the Justices of the Peace Out of Their Sessions: Gathered for the Better Help of Such Justices of Peace as Have Not Been Much Conversant in the Study of the Laws of this Realm: Now Again Enlarged, with Many Precedents and Resolutions of the Quaere's Contained in the Former Impressions*, For the Company of Stationers, 1655

Dance, Daryl C. *From My People: 400 Years of African American Folklore*, W. W. Norton and Company, 2003

Daniels, Cora Linn; Stevans, C. M. *Encyclopedia of Superstitions, Folklore, and the Occult Sciences of the World Collection*, The Minerva Group, Inc., 2003, originally published, 1903

Davies, Owen *America Bewitched: The Story of Witchcraft After Salem*, OUP Oxford, 2013

Davis, Hubert J. *The Silver Bullet, and Other American Witch Stories*, Jonathan David Publishers, 1975

Dickerson Bergen, Fanny; Newell, William Wells *Current Superstitions: Collected from the Oral Tradition of English-Speaking Folk*, American Folk-Lore Society, 1896

Dorson, Richard M. *American Folklore*, University of Chicago

Press, 1977

Dorson, Richard M. *Buying the Wind: Regional Folklore in the United States*, University of Chicago Press, 1964

Drury, Nevill *The Watkins Dictionary of Magic: Over 3,000 Entries on the World of Magical Formulas, Secret Symbols, and the Occult*, Watkins, 2005

Emrich, Duncan *The Folklore of Love and Courtship: The Charms and Divinations, Superstitions and Beliefs, Signs and Prospects of Love, Sweet Love,* American Heritage Press, 1970

Emrich, Duncan *Folklore on the American Land*, Little, Brown, 1972

Emrich, Duncan *The Hodgepodge Book: An Almanac of American Folklore*, Four Winds Press (1972)

Evans-Pritchard, Edward E. *Witchcraft, Oracles and Magic among the Azande* Clarendon Press, 1965

Espinosa, Aurelio M. *The Folklore of Spain in the American Southwest: Traditional Spanish Folk Literature in Northern New Mexico and Southern Colorado,* University of Oklahoma Press, 1990

Feest, Christian F. *Indians of Northeastern North America,* BRILL, 1986

Fischer, David Hackett *Albion's Seed: Four British Folkways in America,* Oxford University Press, 1991

Frazer, Sir James George *The Golden Bough: A Study of Magic and Religion*, Macmillan and Company, 1912

Gainer, Patrick W. *Witches, Ghosts, and Signs, Folklore of the Southern Appalachians,* West Virginia University Press, 2008, kindle edition

Games, Alison *Witchcraft in Early North America,* Rowman and Littlefield, 2012

Gates, Henry Louis and Tatar, Maria *The Annotated African American Folktales (The Annotated Books)*, Liveright Publishing, 2017

Ginzburg, Carlo, *The Night Battles: Witchcraft and Agrarian Cults in the Sixteenth and Seventeenth Centuries*, JHU Press, 2013;

first publishing 1966

Godbeer, Richard *The Devil's Dominion: Magic and Religion in early New England,* Cambridge University Press,1994

Goss, Linda and Barnes, Marian *Talk That Talk: An Anthology of African-American Storytelling,* Simon and Schuster, 1989

Green, Thomas A. *The Greenwood Library of American Folktales,* Greenwood Publishing Group, 2006

Guiley, Rosemary *The Encyclopedia of Witches, Witchcraft & Wicca,* Visionary Living Publishing, 1989

Gunther, Erna *Ethnobotany of Western Washington,* University of Washington Press, 1973

Haase, Donald *The Greenwood Encyclopedia of Folktales and Fairy Tales,* Greenwood Publishing Group, 2007

Halberstein, Robert A., PhD. *Annals of Epidemiology: Medicinal Plants: Historical and Cross-Cultural Usage Patterns,* Elsevier, 2005

Hand, Wayland D. *American Folk Legend: A Symposium,* University of California Press, 1979

Hand, Wayland D. *Popular Beliefs and Superstitions from North Carolina,* Duke University Press, 1964

Hohman, John George *Pow Wows or the Long-lost Friend,* originally published 1828

Hole, Christina *A Mirror of Witchcraft,* Chatto and Windus, 1957

Horowitz, Mitch *Occult America: The Secret History of How Mysticism Shaped Our Nation,* Bantam Books, 2009

Hyatt, Harry Middleton, *Folk-lore from Adams County, Illinois,* Hyatt Foundation, 1965

Indiana Folklore, Volumes 11-13, Indiana University Research Center for the Language Sciences, 1978

Hartlieb, Johannes *The Book of All Forbidden Arts, Superstition, and Sorcery,* 1475

Jordan, Michael *The Green Mantle: An Investigation Into Our Lost Knowledge of Plants,* Cassell, 2001

Kelly, Ruth Edna *The Book of Halloween,* Lothrop, Lee and Shepard

Co., 1919

Kilpatrick, Alan *The Night Has a Naked Soul: Witchcraft and Sorcery Among the Western Cherokee,* Syracuse University Press, 1998

Kittredge, George Lyman *Witchcraft in Old and New England,* Harvard University Press, 1929

Kleen, Michael *Witchcraft in Illinois: A Cultural History,* Arcadia Publishing, 2017

Kramer, Heinrich *Malleus Maleficarum: The Hammer of the Witches,* 1487

Lee, Michele Elizabeth *Working the Roots: Over 400 Years of Traditional African American Healing,* Wadastick, 2017

Levack, Brian P. *The Oxford Handbook of Witchcraft in Early Modern Europe and Colonial America,* OUP Oxford, 2013

Madej-Stang, Adriana *Which Face of Witch: Self-representations of Women as Witches in Works of Contemporary British Women Writers,* Cambridge Scholars Publishing, 2015

Manning, Thomas G. and Burton, Ambrose N. *A Collection of Folklore by Undergraduate Students of East Tennessee State University,* Research Advisory Council, East Tennessee State University, 1966

Michelet, Jules *Satanism and Witchcraft,* Citadel Press edition, 1939

Milnes, Gerald *Signs, Cures, and Witchery: German Appalachian Folklore,* Univ. of Tennessee Press, 2007

Mokgobi, M.G. *Understanding traditional African Healing,* Department of Psychology, School of Health Sciences, Monash South Africa, 2014

Müller-Ebeling, Claudia; Rätsch, Christian; Storl, Wolf-Dieter *Witchcraft Medicine: Healing Arts, Shamanic Practices, and Forbidden Plants,* Simon and Schuster, 2003

Randolph, Vance *Ozark Witchcraft and Folklore,* Columbia University Press, 1947

Simmons, Marc *Witchcraft in the Southwest: Spanish and Indian Supernaturalism on the Rio Grande,* University of Nebraska

Press, 1980

Skinner, Charles M. *Myths and Legends of Our Own Land Vol 2,* Jazzybee Verlag, 2012, 1896

Sullivan, Nancy edited by Hardin, Terri *A Treasury of American Folklore: Our Customs, Beliefs, and Traditions* Barnes and Noble Books; First edition, 1994

The American Folklore Society, *The Journal of American Folklore Collection,* 1888-

The Southern Workman: Volumes 23-24, Hampton Institute., 1894

Tingle, Tim *Spirits Dark and Light: Supernatural Tales from the Five Civilized Tribes,* August House, 2006

Torres, Eliseo "Cheo" *Healing with Herbs and Rituals: A Mexican Tradition,* UNM Press, 2014

Turner, Nancy *Ancient Pathways, Ancestral Knowledge: Ethnobotany and Ecological Wisdom of Indigenous Peoples of Northwestern North America,* McGill-Queen's Press - MQUP, 2014

Wadsworth, Thomson *The Aztecs of Central Mexico: An Imperial Society,* Belmont, CA, 2005

Walker, Deward E. *Witchcraft and Sorcery of the American Native Peoples,* University of Idaho Press, 1989

Weisman, Richard *Witchcraft, Magic, and Religion in 17th-century Massachusetts,* University of Massachusetts Press, 1984

Wehmeyer, Stephen C. *From the Back of the Mirror: "Quicksilver," Tinfoil, and the Shimmer of Sorcery in African-American Vernacular Magic: Magic, Ritual, and Witchcraft, Vol. 12 no. 2,* University of Pennsylvania Press, 2017

White, Thomas *Witches of Pennsylvania: Occult History and Lore,* Arcadia Publishing, 2013

Wilby, Emma *Cunning-Folk and Familiar Spirits: Shamanistic Visionary Traditions in Early Modern British Witchcraft and Magic,* Sussex Academic Press, 2005

Young, William Henry *Buy a Broom Besom: The Story of a Broom,* Treaty-Line Museum, 1976

Recommended Reading

Recommended American Folklore References

The Journal of American Folklore Collection

American Folklore Society Collection

Benjamin Albert Botkin Folklore Collection

Frank C. Brown Collection of North Carolina Folklore

Duncan Emrich Collection

The Green Collection of Folklore

Memoirs of the American Folk Society

Wayland D. Hand Collection

Zora Neale Hurston Collection

Richard Mercer Dorson Collection

Charles G. Leland Collection

Recommended Reading for New World Witch History

America Bewitched: The Story of Witchcraft After Salem by Owen Davies

Witchcraft in Early North America by Alison Games
Witchcraft Myths in American Culture by Marion Gibson

Witches of the Atlantic World: An Historical Reader and Primary Sourcebook by Elaine G. Breslaw

The Witches of Early America by Sally Smith Booth

The Devil's Dominion: Magic and Religion in Early New England by Richard Godbeer

Witchcraft, Magic, and Religion in Seventeenth-Century Massachusetts by Richard Weisman

Black Magic: Religion and the African American Conjuring Tradition by Yvonne P. Chireau

Witchcraft in the Southwest: Spanish and Indian Supernaturalism on the Rio Grande by Marc Simmons

Witchcraft in North Carolina by Tom Peete Cross

Ozark Magic and Folklore by Vance Randolph
Conjure in African American Society by Jeffrey E. Anderson

Recommended Reading for Folk-Witches

Southern Cunning by Aaron Oberon

Besom, Stang & Sword: A Guide to Traditional Witchcraft, the Six-Fold Path & the Hidden Landscape by Christopher Orapello and Tara-Love Maguire

A Deed Without a Name by Lee Morgan

Folk Witchcraft: A Guide to Lore, Land, and the Familiar Spirit for the Solitary Practitioner by Roger J. Horne

Fairycraft: Following The Path of Fairy Witchcraft by Morgan Daimler

About the Author

The Riverton Witch, Via Hedera, is a Southern-California born folklorist, occult researcher, essayist and sculptor currently based out of the South Seattle region. Raised in an ethnically and religiously diverse family deeply rooted in social justice, she has spent her life tracing the folklore and superstitions of her many ancestors across the world. Via's writing focuses on traditional witchcraft practices, American folklore, animism and green-spirituality. She offers and produces commission altar sculptures as well as private classes on cartomancy and traditional witchcraft. In her down-time, she works as college Event Coordinator, herds unruly rabbits, haunts local pubs and jams to The Eagles.

www.viahedera.com

**MOON
BOOKS**

PAGANISM & SHAMANISM

What is Paganism? A religion, a spirituality, an alternative belief system, nature worship? You can find support for all these definitions (and many more) in dictionaries, encyclopaedias, and text books of religion, but subscribe to any one and the truth will evade you. Above all Paganism is a creative pursuit, an encounter with reality, an exploration of meaning and an expression of the soul. Druids, Heathens, Wiccans and others, all contribute their insights and literary riches to the Pagan tradition. Moon Books invites you to begin or to deepen your own encounter, right here, right now.

If you have enjoyed this book, why not tell other readers by posting a review on your preferred book site.

Recent bestsellers from Moon Books are:

Journey to the Dark Goddess
How to Return to Your Soul
Jane Meredith
Discover the powerful secrets of the Dark Goddess and
transform your depression, grief and pain into healing
and integration.
Paperback: 978-1-84694-677-6 ebook: 978-1-78099-223-5

Shamanic Reiki
Expanded Ways of Working with Universal Life Force Energy
Llyn Roberts, Robert Levy
Shamanism and Reiki are each powerful ways of healing; together,
their power multiplies. *Shamanic Reiki* introduces techniques to
help healers and Reiki practitioners tap ancient healing wisdom.
Paperback: 978-1-84694-037-8 ebook: 978-1-84694-650-9

Pagan Portals – The Awen Alone
Walking the Path of the Solitary Druid
Joanna van der Hoeven
An introductory guide for the solitary Druid, *The Awen Alone* will
accompany you as you explore, and seek out your own place
within the natural world.
Paperback: 978-1-78279-547-6 ebook: 978-1-78279-546-9

A Kitchen Witch's World of Magical Herbs & Plants
Rachel Patterson
A journey into the magical world of herbs and plants, filled with
magical uses, folklore, history and practical magic. By popular
writer, blogger and kitchen witch, Tansy Firedragon.
Paperback: 978-1-78279-621-3 ebook: 978-1-78279-620-6

Medicine for the Soul
The Complete Book of Shamanic Healing
Ross Heaven
All you will ever need to know about shamanic healing and how to
become your own shaman…
Paperback: 978-1-78099-419-2 ebook: 978-1-78099-420-8

Shaman Pathways – The Druid Shaman
Exploring the Celtic Otherworld
Danu Forest
A practical guide to Celtic shamanism with exercises and
techniques as well as traditional lore for exploring the Celtic
Otherworld.
Paperback: 978-1-78099-615-8 ebook: 978-1-78099-616-5

Traditional Witchcraft for the Woods and Forests
A Witch's Guide to the Woodland with Guided Meditations and
Pathworking
Mélusine Draco
A Witch's guide to walking alone in the woods, with guided
meditations and pathworking.
Paperback: 978-1-84694-803-9 ebook: 978-1-84694-804-6

Wild Earth, Wild Soul
A Manual for an Ecstatic Culture
Bill Pfeiffer
Imagine a nature-based culture so alive and so connected,
spreading like wildfire. This book is the first flame…
Paperback: 978-1-78099-187-0 ebook: 978-1-78099-188-7

Naming the Goddess

Trevor Greenfield

Naming the Goddess is written by over eighty adherents and scholars of Goddess and Goddess Spirituality.

Paperback: 978-1-78279-476-9 ebook: 978-1-78279-475-2

Shapeshifting into Higher Consciousness

Heal and Transform Yourself and Our World with Ancient Shamanic and Modern Methods

Llyn Roberts

Ancient and modern methods that you can use every day to transform yourself and make a positive difference in the world.

Paperback: 978-1-84694-843-5 ebook: 978-1-84694-844-2

Readers of ebooks can buy or view any of these bestsellers by clicking on the live link in the title. Most titles are published in paperback and as an ebook. Paperbacks are available in traditional bookshops. Both print and ebook formats are available online.

Find more titles and sign up to our readers' newsletter at
http://www.johnhuntpublishing.com/paganism
Follow us on Facebook at https://www.facebook.com/MoonBooks
and Twitter at https://twitter.com/MoonBooksJHP